YORK N

General Editors: P
of Stirling) & Profess...
University of Beirut)

William Shakespeare

SONNETS

Notes by Geoffrey M. Ridden

BA M PHIL (LEEDS)
Head of Student Services,
King Alfred's College, Winchester

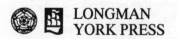

LONGMAN
YORK PRESS

YORK PRESS
Immeuble Esseily, Place Riad Solh, Beirut.

ADDISON WESLEY LONGMAN LIMITED
Edinburgh Gate, Harlow,
Essex CM20 2JE, England
Associated companies, branches and representatives
throughout the world

© Librairie du Liban 1982

First published 1982
Eleventh impression 1997

ISBN 0-582-78285-6

Produced by Longman Singapore Publishers Pte Ltd
Printed in Singapore

Contents

Contents

Part 1

Introduction

William Shakespeare

The baptism of William Shakespeare was recorded on 26 April 1564 in Stratford, England. It is reasonable to assume that he was born not more than a few days before that date. His father, John Shakespeare, was a prominent local citizen who held some of the most important positions in the government of the town. William probably attended Stratford grammar school, but unlike most other writers of the time, he did not proceed to university. In 1582 he married Anne Hathaway, eight years his senior, and they had three children, the eldest a girl, Susanna, and twins Hamnet and Judith.

We do not know when or for what reason Shakespeare left Stratford for London, but it is clear that he had established a reputation for himself by 1592 when Robert Greene (1558–92), a playwright with a university background, warned his learned colleagues against:

> an upstart crow, beautified with our feathers, that with his *Tiger's heart wrapt in a Player's hide* supposes he is as well able to bombast out a blank verse as the best of you; and being an absolute *Johannes fac totum* is in his own conceit the only Shake-scene in a country.*

It is clear from this attack that Shakespeare was already well-known both as an actor and a playwright. The following year he published a narrative poem, *Venus and Adonis*, which further enhanced his reputation. He became a shareholder in the theatrical company with which he worked and enjoyed financial as well as professional success, sufficient to allow him to buy one of the largest houses in Stratford in 1597. None of his contemporary rival playwrights is known to have had a share in the profits of a playhouse.

The popularity of Shakespeare's plays is indicated by the description given in *Palladis Tamia: Wit's Treasury* in 1598 by Francis Meres (1565–1647), a Cambridge scholar who was living in London from 1597 to 1598, who says that they are 'the most excellent in both kinds' (that is, in both tragedies and comedies). Although Shakespeare is not the only playwright mentioned by Meres, he is the only one to have his

---

* *Greene's Groatsworth of Wit*, quoted in *William Shakespeare: The Complete Works*, edited by Peter Alexander, Collins, London, 1951, p.xvi.

plays listed. Furthermore, after 1598, with the publication of *Love's Labour's Lost*, copies of Shakespeare's plays were regularly published with his name on the title-page, a very rare phenomenon at that time, and perhaps indicative again of his popularity.

It is not easy to provide accurate dates for all of Shakespeare's thirty-seven plays, but it seems likely that most of his comedies and history plays were written before 1600, that he wrote his great tragedies between 1601 and 1608, and that a small group of plays requiring more elaborate stage-effects (*Pericles*, *Cymbeline*, *The Winter's Tale* and *The Tempest*) was written after the company transferred to a different theatre in 1608.

In the last years of his life, Shakespeare lived in retirement in Stratford and he died on 23 April 1616. His wife was buried next to him in 1623.

Shakespeare the poet

There can be no doubt that Shakespeare is generally regarded as the greatest playwright who ever lived. Throughout the world his plays continue to be performed, and memorable lines from them have slipped almost unnoticed into everyday use. Shakespeare's dramatic genius, although not widely recognised by his near-contemporaries, was, however, acclaimed well before he was recognised as a great poet. F.E. Halliday, reviewing criticism of Shakespeare across three and a half centuries, comments with some surprise:

> It is remarkable that, apart from contemporaries and near-contemporaries like Ben Johnson and Milton, no critic before Coleridge seems to have been aware that Shakespeare was before all else a poet.... Shakespeare was a poet before he was a dramatist, and it is possible that he turned playwright only, or at least mainly, from economic motives.*

Although the dating of much of Shakespeare's work is uncertain and it may not be the case that he turned from poems to plays quite in the manner suggested by Halliday, it is true that his first published work was *Venus and Adonis*, published in 1593 and reprinted fifteen times before 1640. Although *Henry the Sixth Part II* and *Henry the Sixth Part III* may have been written and performed before *Venus and Adonis*, they did not appear in print until 1594 and 1595 respectively. In this sense, then, Shakespeare was indeed a poet before he became a dramatist.

Francis Meres wrote in *Palladis Tamia*:

* F.E. Halliday, *Shakespeare and his Critics*, Duckworth, London, 1949, p.21.

the sweete wittie soule of *Ouid* lives in mellifluous hony-tongued Shakespeare, witnes his *Venus* and *Adonis*, his *Lucrece*, his sugred Sonnets among his private friends, &c.*

Meres goes on to speak of the excellences of Shakespeare's plays, but his eulogy begins with a reference to Shakespeare's poems. Similar praise of the poems is to be found in Richard Barnfield's *Poems in Divers Humors* (1598) and John Weaver's *Epigrammes in the Oldest Cut, and newest Fashion* (1599).

Although for most of us our first acquaintance with Shakespeare will be with the dramatic works, we can hardly fail to perceive the extent to which these plays gain their effect through the sheer poetry of the language. Consider, for example, this description of Cordelia in *King Lear*:

> You have seen
> Sunshine and rain at once: her smiles and tears
> Were like a better way. Those happy smilets
> That play'd on her ripe lips seem'd not to know
> What guests were in her eyes, which parted thence
> As pearls from diamonds dropp'd.   (IV, iii, 17–22)

We realise that these lines could only have been written by a dramatist who was also a practised poet. This description evokes perfectly the positive qualities of balance and order which Shakespeare wants us to appreciate in Cordelia. Her tears are precious, and the blend of tears and smiles is spiritual and heavenly. This is a description of confused and conflicting emotions, but the emotions are held in check and under control. There is no sense of Cordelia allowing her passions to rule her, nor of any wildness in her behaviour. This use of language is genuinely poetic in that it expresses order and control through imagery and the careful positioning of words. The controlled use of language to express and define even extreme emotions is most characteristic of the sonnet form.

The sonnet

Of all the standard poetic forms, the sonnet appears most easily defined. The *Oxford English Dictionary* cites only two meanings for the word, one defining primarily its form, the other its content:

(1) A piece of verse (properly expressive of one main idea) consisting of fourteen decasyllabic lines, with rhymes arranged according to one or other of certain definite schemes.

---

* Quoted in F.E. Halliday, *Shakespeare and his Critics*, p.45. The reference to sonnets is not necessarily an allusion to the sonnet sequence with which we are concerned.

(2) A short poem or piece of verse; in early use especially one of a lyrical and amatory character.

These two meanings encapsulate the basis of the sonnet in Shakespeare's time: sonnets were then primarily love poems (although later writers, including Milton, put the form to other uses), and they were normally written in a rigid structure comprising fourteen lines, each of ten syllables.

The sonnet form was initiated and established in Italy over three hundred years before Shakespeare. The first sonnets were written in 1230 by a Sicilian lawyer, Giacomo da Lentimo, but it was Petrarch (Francesco Petrarca, 1304–74) who was responsible for the great popularity of the form. In old age he rearranged the poems he had written for his beloved Laura into a sequence called the *Rime* or *Canzoniere*. The structure of the sonnet was largely established in this sequence, although the English form of the sonnet made significant deviations from its Italian model.

Italian sonnets did not have a simple unity. The early sonneteers divided their sonnets into two unequal parts: an eight-line section (the octave) and a six-line section (the sestet). It is this division which gives sonnets their structure: they are symmetrical, and very often there is a turning-point at the beginning of the ninth line, announcing a new section. This sonnet by Sir Philip Sidney (1554–86) demonstrates the division into octave and sestet, and the turning-point at the beginning of line 9:

> You that do search for everie purling spring,
> Which from the ribs of old *Parnassus* flowes,
> And everie floure, not sweet perhaps, which growes
> Neare therabout, into your Poesie wring;
> You that do Dictionarie's methods bring
> Into your rimes, running in ratling rowes;
> You that poore *Petrarch's* long-deceased woes
> With new-borne sighes and denisend wit do sing:
> You take wrong waies, those far-set helpes be such,
> As do bewray a want of inward tuch:
> And sure at length stolne goods do come to light;
> But if (both for your love and skill) your name
> You seeke to nurse at fullest breasts of Fame,
> *Stella* behold, and then begin to endite.*

In the first eight lines of this sonnet Sidney identifies certain kinds of poets who seek to find inspiration by reading the works of other

---

* *The Poems of Sir Philip Sidney*, edited by William A. Ringler, Jr., Oxford University Press, London, 1962, p.172.

writers. In line 9 a new movement starts as he tells them in a forthright manner that they are in error ('You take wrong ways') and thus the poem concludes with Sidney's view of where true poetic inspiration lies: in his beloved Stella.

This division in meaning between octave and sestet is reinforced by other divisions, in punctuation and in rhyme-scheme. The octave is arranged into one clause of emphatic four lines (ending in a semi-colon), and two clauses each of two lines (ending in a semi-colon and a colon respectively). The sestet has only one break at the end of a line (the semi-colon at the end of line 11) and thus falls into three-line units. This difference between octave and sestet is mirrored in the rhyme-scheme: the rhyme words (spring-wring-bring-sing; flows-grows-rows-woes; such-touch; name-fame; light-endite) occur in the following pattern:

OCTAVE		SESTET	
a b b a	a b b a	c c d	e e d
quatrain	quatrain	tercet	tercet

The groupings of four lines within the octave are called quatrains: the groups of three lines within the sestet are known as tercets. Sidney, in this sonnet, is using the form in a very similar fashion to that employed by Petrarch. Notice, however, the way in which Sidney is demonstrating his mastery of the form. It would have been very simple for him to have arranged his argument neatly to fit the rhyme-scheme: eight lines for his proposition, six lines for his conclusion; but Sidney is more subtle than that. Although his rhyme-scheme gives him two quatrains in the octave, he does not produce two equally weighted statements. Instead we have one four-line statement (lines 1–4), a two-line statement (5–6), then another two-line statement (7–8). Furthermore, although the argument turns at the beginning of line 9, it does not turn simply by rejecting what has gone before. Many sonneteers mark the turn quite clearly by beginning line 9 with 'But' or 'Yet', but Sidney does something quite different here: he begins line 9 in exactly the same way that he began line 1, line 5, and line 7. It appears for a moment as if there is to be no turn at all, but Sidney is achieving the turn by use of rhythm. Line 9 is marked off from the rest of the sonnet by the inclusion of that strong, emphatic four-syllable clause: 'You take wrong ways'.

Part of the effect of this sonnet comes from Sidney's ability to establish a tension between the various patterns within the poem: the meaning, the punctuation, and the rhyme-scheme. The three patterns do not coincide in every respect and thus the sonnet holds our interest and does not become merely routine.

Petrarch's sonnets influenced Chaucer (1340–1400) and he included a translation of Petrarch's sonnet 88 in his *Troilus and Criseyde*.

However, the translation is not itself in the form of a sonnet and the honour of producing the first sonnet in English goes to Sir Thomas Wyatt (1503–42). As a diplomat and traveller Wyatt came across the writings of Petrarch and of French sonneteers, and he set about developing an equivalent form in English. Like those of his contemporary, Henry Howard, Earl of Surrey (1517–47), Wyatt's sonnets are, for the most part, translations or imitations of those of Petrarch. However, because Italian and English are different kinds of languages, some developments from the original Italian form were inevitable. One development merits particular attention.

Wyatt, in the sestets of his imitations of Petrarch, favoured rhyme-scheme c d d c e e which might be expected to set apart the last two lines. Because of the punctuation of these lines, the effect is still to preserve the sense of a full sestet. This is an example:

Who list her hunt (I put him out of doubt)
As well as I may spend his time in vain.
And graven with diamonds in letters plain
There is written her fair neck round about:
'Noli me tangere, for Caesar's I am,
And wild for to hold, though I seem tame.'*

Surrey, however, developed the sestet even further so that its final two lines served not as a conclusion to the sestet but as a separate entity, a rhyming couplet summing up the sonnet as a whole. Thus the form of the sonnet was changed: it no longer necessarily had the proportions eight to six, but something much more like twelve to two. So popular did the use of this final couplet become that it established itself as a trademark of the English sonnet. George Gascoigne (1525–77) clearly felt that it was the norm:

Then you have Sonnets, . . . which are of fourtene lynes, every line conteyning tenne syllables. The first twelve do ryme in staves of four lines by crosse meetre, and the last two ryming togither do conclude the whole.†

Gascoigne exaggerates somewhat, in that the use of a final couplet was not as universal as he would imply. Nevertheless, this modification of the sonnet meant that English poets could choose from a greater range of possible sonnet forms than ever before, and could place their turning-points at line 9, at line 13, or, as in this sonnet by Sidney, in both of these:

* *Silver Poets of the Sixteenth Century*, edited by Gerald Bullett, Dent, London, 1947, p.3.
† Quoted in J. Fuller, *The Sonnet*, Methuen, London, 1972, p.15.

Having this day my horse, my hand, my launce
Guided as well, that I obtain'd the prize,
Both by the judgement of the English eyes
And of some sent from that sweet enemie Fraunce;
Horsemen my skill in horsemanship advaunce;
Towne-folkes my strength; a daintier judge applies
His praise to sleight, which from good use doth rise;
Some luckie wits impute it but to chaunce;
Others, because of both sides I do take
My bloud from them, who did excell in this,
Think Nature me a man of armes did make.
How farre they shoote awrie! the true cause is,
Stella lookt on, and from her heavenly face
Sent forth the beames, which made so faire my race.*

Writing of this sonnet, John Fuller points out that it is possible to see either a contrast between octave and sestet (Sidney's abilities as a horseman and his true motivation) or a contrast between three quatrains (the first dealing with his success, the second explaining it through his education, the third explaining it through Nature) and a final couplet which provides the solution.†

The sonnet form which Shakespeare inherited was a sophisticated and developed literary mode capable of great flexibility in spite of its apparently rigid structure.

Sonnet sequences

Although Petrarch's sonnets were woven together into a narrative sequence, Wyatt and Surrey did not adopt this aspect of the form. Their sonnets (published in *Tottel's Miscellany*, 1557) were individual, separate entities and cannot be said to have led to the popularity of sonneteering in Elizabethan England. The real turning-point came with the publication of Sir Philip Sidney's sonnet sequence *Astrophil and Stella* in 1591. In this sequence Sidney adopted not only the form of the sonnet but also further Petrarchan conventions, including the use of a sequence of sonnets to investigate the developments and fluctuations in his relationship with his beloved, Stella. *Astrophil and Stella* was widely imitated in the last years of the sixteenth century when the vogue for sonnet sequences was at its height. In many respects Shakespeare's sonnet sequence marks the end of that particular literary fashion. Kenneth Muir writes: 'Shakespeare's choice of the sonnet form was dictated by its popularity in the last decade of the sixteenth

* *The Poems of Sir Philip Sidney*, p.185.
† J. Fuller, *The Sonnet*, Methuen, London, 1972, p.18–19.

century. If he had been born a generation earlier or a generation later, he would not have written sonnets.'*

In *Astrophil and Stella* Sidney writes of a relationship between a man (Astrophil, meaning star-lover) and an unattainable lady (Stella, meaning star). We know that Sidney himself had loved a lady, Penelope Devereux, who eventually married another man, but we should be wrong to take all of *Astrophil and Stella* as autobiography. Sidney is aware of the extent to which he is using literary convention and often conveys this knowledge in a wryly humorous manner. In sonnet 15, discussed in detail earlier, Sidney is deriding those poets who imitate Petrarch slavishly, describing Petrarch's passion and not their own. His conclusion is that true inspiration can come only from writing about Stella. However, there is an inherent paradox here: Sidney is inviting all poets to derive inspiration from his beloved, and yet, if they did, their poems could not escape being as insincere as if they were inspired by Petrarch's Laura. The best of the sonneteers, including Sidney and Shakespeare, were aware of both the extent to which they were employing conventions and the contribution of their own originality. The opening sonnet in Sidney's sequence declares that he will reject convention and artifice, and will write instead spontaneously, from the heart; and yet he writes in the sonnet form, a medium far from natural or spontaneous.

Many of the Petrarchan conventions used by Sidney and the Elizabethan sonneteers are concerned with the nature of the relationship between the poet and his beloved, and some of these conventions are to be found not only in sonnets but in other love-literature of the medieval and renaissance period. In this tradition the lover writes of his lady, without any hope of attaining her. She may be married to another or there may be a social obstacle to their liaison, but always the love is hopeless. Indeed, in none of the sonnets cited so far does the poet address the lady directly: in all cases she is referred to in the third person.

Since the love is unattainable, the lady can be portrayed as pure and undefiled. Although at times she may appear cruel in rejecting the advances of the lover, the lover would not wish her to surrender herself to him because that would lower her in his estimation. This is one of the paradoxes fundamental to the Petrarchan tradition: the lover begs for her love yet does not wish her to surrender. The language of the sonnets is full of such paradoxes: the lady is beautiful yet cruel; desirable but chaste; the lover suffers yet does not wish his suffering to end; he wants his lady to mourn his absence, but does not want her to suffer.

Every aspect of a love relationship can be explored in the sonnet

---

* K. Muir, *Shakespeare's Sonnets*, Allen and Unwin, London, 1979, p.44.

sequence, except one: the consummation of the relationship. The poet may describe how he met the lady and how he fell in love with her immediately and hopelessly. He may describe her beauty by means of ingenious comparisons and then will tell us remarkably little about the details of her actual appearance. According to the convention the lady will be 'fair' and we learn little else of her. Indeed, although a sequence like *Astrophil and Stella* may appear to be a detailed investigation of the stages of a relationship, it is firmly centred on the man: it is his thoughts we hear, his reactions that are revealed; no other voice is heard but that of the lover. We learn of his love, his pain, his delight, his jealousy (always of a rival lover, never of a husband); the feelings of the lady are left unexplored.

In writing of his love in a sonnet sequence the poet is pursuing an ideal. In many sequences the love for the lady turns into a spiritual quest for a better, more perfect love: the love of God. The effect of the love on the man is to ennoble him and to turn his thoughts to a spiritual plane. This is one reason why the Petrarchan sonneteer expects no physical consummation of his love: the love must remain pure and idealised. Another reason is, of course, that the interest of the reader is maintained only as long as the pursuit continues; if the lover wins his lady dynamism disappears from his sequence.

The following sonnet by Sidney demonstrates the use of the Petrarchan convention of an idealised, pure love. Typically, however, Sidney moves beyond this convention by asking in a most un-Petrarchan way for his lady's surrender: the sonnet turns its argument in the final line:

Who will in fairest booke of Nature know,
How Vertue may best lodg'd in beautie be,
Let him but learne of *Love* to reade in thee
Stella, those faire lines, which true goodnesse show.
There shall he find all vices' overthrow,
Not by rude force, but sweetest soveraigntie
Of reason, from whose light those night-birds flie;
That inward sunne in thine eyes shineth so.
And not content to be Perfection's heire
Thy selfe, doest strive all minds that way to move,
Who marke in thee what is in thee most faire.
So while thy beautie drawes the heart to love,
As fast thy Vertue bends that love to good:
'But ah,' Desire still cries, 'give me some food.'*

---

* *The Poems of Sir Philip Sidney*, p.201.

Convention and originality

The twentieth century places a great deal of emphasis on originality in all popular western art forms. Innovations in technique as well as in subject matter tend to be widely praised, and any form of imitation is derided and rejected. This delight in novelty is a relatively recent phenomenon and certainly not one which would have gained the approval of renaissance writers.

One of the major aims of writers in the period from 1580 to 1670 was to establish the worth of English literature and its comparable status with the great classical literature of the past. Petrarch and his contemporaries established that it was possible to write good poetry in Italian and, gradually, the potentials of other vernacular literatures were explored. It was felt essential, however, to demonstrate that these modern languages could cope with the standard classical literary genres: tragedy, epic, lyric, pastoral, elegy. Thus Edmund Spenser (1552–99) in his unfinished work *The Faerie Queene* is attempting to prove that English is a fit language for epic poetry. In writing sonnets and working within a framework of convention, English poets could exhibit their mastery of the basis of poetic technique. This was felt to be infinitely better than attempting to develop new poetic genres. Indeed, the poet who is arguably the greatest and most inventive poet in the English language, John Milton (1608–74), wrote entirely within poetic forms inherited from his predecessors.

Even within the sonnet form there was considerable flexibility and opportunity for the display of individuality. Sidney, in the sonnet quoted above, is demonstrating both his awareness of the convention and his ability to move beyond it, and even the early sonneteers such as Wyatt are no mere translators. Wyatt, for example, takes Petrarch's sonnet 190 and produces a version which subtly departs from the original to give a very different conclusion, one more relevant to Wyatt's own situation.

Within the situations described in a sonnet sequence there are inevitably standard, universal features. All lovers must part on occasions and we may feel in reading a sonnet by Petrarch, or Sidney, or Shakespeare, that the poet is expressing emotions which we have felt ourselves. The great poet will read a sonnet by a predecessor and will be able not only to relate its sentiments to his own experiences, but to express those sentiments in a unique and personal way. A basic requirement in this expression was for the poet to subsume his own identity by taking on another role, becoming a different person. We are familiar enough with the concept in drama: few readers of Shakespeare's plays would assume that the sentiments expressed by the characters are those of Shakespeare himself. However, the assumption is often made that sonnet sequences are autobiographical, that they either describe felt emotions and real incident or else are pale copies of a Petrarchan original. Critics at the beginning of this century were, in fact, distressed to discover the extent of Sidney's debt to Petrarch and swift to censure him for it. Now, however, a less extreme view prevails, in which it is appreciated that Sidney and Shakespeare are using the methods of good dramatic poets, demonstrating a mastery of the sonnet form by creating such credible portraits of poet-lovers. Hamlet is described by Ophelia as a lover and a poet, and yet we do not assume that every word spoken by Hamlet expresses Shakespeare's own views. We would be wise to exercise similar caution in equating poets in sonnet sequences with the authors of those sequences.

Patronage, poetry, and Shakespeare's sonnets

A characteristic of the sonnet sequences of both Sidney and Shakespeare is that both deal not only with love but with the role of poetry itself in conveying emotion. Each refers to the difficulties faced by a poet in attempting to write within a prescribed convention, but Shakespeare has other interests not shared by Sidney, who, for all his skill as a poet, was an amateur who did not earn his living from writing. Shakespeare, not a gentleman by birth like Sidney, was a professional writer and this very professionalism underlies his sonnet sequence.

In order to earn his living from his pen Shakespeare had to either write for the stage, a lucrative popular market, or find a patron who would support him in more serious writing. The comment from Greene quoted earlier (p.5) indicates the reactions of a university man to Shakespeare the popular dramatist. Only by seeking patronage could a writer safeguard his reputation from this kind of attack, the stigma of seeking vulgar fame and fortune.

Shakespeare was by no means the first English poet to seek the help of a patron. Spenser dedicated *The Faerie Queene* to Elizabeth, but added seventeen sonnets of praise to various distinguished gentlemen. Shakespeare dedicated his first published work, *Venus and Adonis*, to the Earl of Southampton, and his second published poem, *The Rape of Lucrece*, includes this fulsome dedication to that same patron:

> The love I dedicate to your Lordship is without end; Whereof this Pamphlet without beginning is but a superfluous Moity. The warrant I have of your honourable disposition, not the worth of my untutored lines makes it assured of acceptance. What I have done is yours, what I hauve to doe is yours, being part in all I have, denoted yours. Were my worth greater, my duety would shew greater, meane time, as it is, it is bound to your Lordship . . . *

* Quoted in F.E. Halliday, *Shakespeare and his Critics*, p.320.

This kind of praise, full of balance and contrast, looks very similar indeed to the language used by poets to address their ladies. Shakespeare here, dwelling upon his inferiority and unworthiness, writes in a similar vein to that used by the lover to his mistress. It could well be that this dedication gave Shakespeare the idea of writing a sonnet sequence in which the patron was to play a prominent role.

If this dedication is compared with the dedication to *Venus and Adonis* it may appear that a shift has occurred in the relationship between poet and patron. The dedication to the earlier work is little more than a plea for money and lacks the expression of love found in the dedication to *The Rape of Lucrece*, and critics have attempted, on the basis of this slender evidence, to reconstruct the nature of the relationship between Shakespeare and his patron. There is remarkably little evidence about this patronage, as Schoenbaum's biography wisely concludes, although it has generated a mythology of its own. What is certain is that Shakespeare did not explicitly dedicate his sonnets to the Earl of Southampton. We shall investigate in a later section the claims for regarding the mysterious Mr. W.H. referred to in the dedication of the sonnets as possibly being Southampton, but it might be worth observing that Shakespeare could, if he had wanted to, have been more explicit in the dedication. The fact that the dedication of Shakespeare's sonnets is so cryptic might be a further indication of the fact that Shakespeare did not wish the narrative expressed in the sonnets to be too closely identified with his own life.

Shakespeare deals with patronage in a later work, *Timon of Athens*, probably written in 1608, in which the wealthy central character finally betrayed by his friends is initially flattered by, among others, a Poet. The Poet is clearly working under the patronage of Timon and his poem is a eulogy in his praise. However much it may seem that Timon's folly merits empty flattery, an audience cannot but feel that literary patronage is being presented unfavourably in the opening scene of this play. As an institution it seems not to have worked successfully in reality and Shakespeare was not alone in pointing to its defects: a poet could all too easily slip into insincere and hollow flattery merely to gain his patron's favour.

Alvin B. Kernan* has recently suggested that Shakespeare's entire sonnet sequence may be an account of the poet's dissatisfaction with the system of patronage. Kernan sees the sequence as expressing the poet's growing awareness of the world; his increasing self-consciousness about the nature and function of poetry; his dissatisfaction with the social status of the poet; his gradual move from patronage

---

* Alvin B. Kernan, *The Playwright as Magician*, Yale University Press, New Haven and London, 1979.

to the theatre. Kernan may go rather too far in characterising the Dark Lady as the muse of the theatre, but his thesis is valuable in drawing attention to the extent to which the sonnets are about the profession of the writer and the social circumstances surrounding that profession.

A note on the text

There are many texts available for all of Shakespeare's works. Definitive editions of the sonnets are, however, hard to come by. The editor of the Arden edition òf the sonnets has not yet completed her labours, and the New Penguin edition of the poems is similarly unpublished. These Notes should ideally be used with Stephen Booth's edition, *Shakespeare's Sonnets*, Yale University Press, New Haven and London, 1977, which has the advantage of providing facsimiles of the first edition of the sonnets alongside a version using modernised spelling. It should prove possible, however, to use the Notes with any text of the sonnets, provided the text adheres to the ordering of the first edition. For ease of reference all sonnets are referred to by Arabic numerals rather than the Roman equivalents.

Part 2

Summaries
of SHAKESPEARE'S SONNETS

A general summary

There has been much controversy over the ordering of Shakespeare's sonnet sequence and certain critics have chosen to regard the sonnets as a huge jigsaw puzzle which could be put together in a variety of different ways by different readers to provide alternative narrative lines. It is tempting to consider alternative ordering, but the temptation is probably best avoided. The generally accepted order, that of the first edition of 1609, provides a skeleton of a narrative, much looser and less well-defined than contemporary sequences by other sonneteers.

Of the 154 sonnets, the final two can be disregarded as separate from the rest of the sequence and, indeed, Shakespeare's authorship of these two sonnets has been questioned. The major division in the sonnet sequence occurs at sonnet 127 where a new movement is heralded: the first 126 sonnets are concerned with the poet's relationship with a young man, his patron and social superior. In this group there are also references to a rival poet and to the poet's own mistress. From sonnet 127 onwards the central character is no longer the young man, but a Dark Lady. Although the narrative sequence of Shakespeare's sonnets may be less clear than contemporary sequences, his use of linkage from one sonnet to another is more extensive than that of any of his predecessors. In *Tears of Fancie* (1593), Thomas Watson (*c.* 1557–92) had included some linkage between sonnets, but Shakespeare develops this to a high degree of sophistication.

Detailed summaries

Detailed summaries are presented of groups of sonnets. There is no attempt to paraphrase individual sonnets, since this task would be quite impossible: any sonnet will say much more than a paraphrase could contain. The brief account of each sonnet is followed by glosses and notes on specific words and phrases.

Sonnets 1–17

This group is the most clearly linked set of sonnets within the sequence. Its overriding theme is that the young man, beautiful though he is, is vulnerable to the passage of time and that his beauty needs to be preserved either by his producing a child who will duplicate his beauty, or through the poet's own description of that beauty.

Sonnet 1
The principal images are the flower (symbolising beauty) and feeding (the need for all living things to be nourished).

increase:	future generations
tender heir:	this suggests the vulnerability of a child, as well as the poet's affection for the young man
contracted:	promised in marriage
self-substantial fuel:	fuel of your own making (an image of the candle fed by its own wax)
to thy sweet self too cruel:	a paradox: conventionally the beloved would be cruel to the poet; here the young man is cruel to himself
gaudy:	joyous
buriest:	both confine and kill
content:	complacency, and inner self
churl:	young boy
niggarding:	acting as a miser
this glutton be:	you will become this kind of glutton
the world's due:	what should be due to the world

Sonnet 2
The sonnet continues the image of beauty as a treasure, using images of beauty as clothing (something external and subject to wear) and of commerce (the child, introduced here for the first time, as the total of his account).

besiege:	attack
field:	battlefield
livery:	uniform (of a soldier or a servant)
tattered weed:	worn piece of clothing
lusty days:	time of youth
all-eating:	all-consuming
sum my count:	be the total of my account
proving:	all the sonnets are essentially proving a case, often quite legalistically
This were:	this would be
see:	feel, and, literally, see your son

Sonnet 3
Another plea for the young man to produce an heir. The principal image is that of the mirror: this shows the young man his face, reminds him of mortality, reminds him of his resemblance to his mother, and of the possibility of his renewing his beauty with an heir.

glass:	mirror
form another:	create another face by having a baby
beguile:	cheat
unbless:	fail to make fortunate (by failing to make pregnant)
unear'd:	unploughed, unfertilised
tillage:	ploughing (an image of sexual intercourse)
husbandry:	a pun: both farming and the state of being a husband
posterity:	future generations
glass:	visual image
Calls back:	remembers
windows of thine age:	meaning both through the perspective given by age, and through the spectacles worn by old people

Sonnet 4

This sonnet reverts to the image of beauty as wealth, in this case a legacy given by Nature to be spent. The young man is again presented (as he is in sonnet 1) as a miser unwilling to share his beauty.

Unthrifty:	profitless
gives nothing ... lend:	merely lends, does not give permanently
free:	generous
largess:	generosity
Profitless usurer:	a paradox: a usurer is in business to make a profit
live:	defeat death, produce an heir
traffic:	business dealings, sexual dealings
gone:	dead
acceptable audit:	the traditional biblical metaphor, that when we die we are called to account for our behaviour
which used ... be:	which, if used, would produced a life who could be your executor

Sonnet 5

This sonnet deals explicitly with the work of time which undoes the beauty which it creates. The image used to express the defeat of time's destruction is the distilling of flowers into perfume, thus preserving their essence though losing their external beauty.

And that unfair:	and make that ugly
confounds:	defeats
o'ersnowed:	snowed upon, made white with age
were not ... left:	if the perfume of summer flowers were not left
Beauty's ... bereft:	the effect of beauty would die as quickly as beauty itself
Leese:	lose

Sonnet 6

This continues the image of the distillation of perfume, urging the young man to act in a similar fashion by having an heir. Again it uses images of trade and usury (like sonnet 4).

Then:	this signals that the sonnet continues an idea begun in the previous sonnet
ragged:	rough
vial:	vessel (with a possible pun on vile)
happies those:	makes those happy
refigured:	recalculated, and made your figure again
self-willed:	stubborn (a pun on Shakespeare's name, Will?)
make worms thine heir:	allow yourself to be consumed by worms

Sonnet 7

This sonnet is dominated by a new image not previously used, that of beauty as the sun, impressive as it rises but less regarded as it sets.

Lo:	behold (a poetic word)
the gracious light:	the sun
each under eye:	each inferior eye
pilgrimage:	journey through the day
car:	the chariot of the sun
reeleth:	staggers
outgoing:	passing on from
son:	a pun on sun (the word itself is not used in the sonnet)

Sonnet 8

This sonnet is built partly on the paradox that the young man, though music in himself, is made sad by music. It develops this notion into a contrast between the man's single state and the harmony of music, based on combinations of notes. A similar analogy of music and social order appears in *Troilus and Cressida*, Act I, Scene 3, lines 109–10.

Music ... hear:	you, who are music to listen to
war not:	do not disagree
thine annoy:	what annoys you
concord:	harmony, marriage
who ... singleness:	you who work against harmony by remaining single
the parts ... bear:	both the roles which you should play in life (husband/father) and the musical line which you ought to sing
one string ... another:	the strings of a lute are tuned in pairs
speechless song:	song without words
being many, seeming one:	a description of the effect of harmony in music

Sonnet 9
The poet suggests that the young man may be remaining single so that he will leave no widow to mourn for him. He argues that the world will mourn the death of the young man if he dies without an heir. The images of commerce are linked with those in earlier sonnets.

consum'st thyself:	a reference back to sonnet 1
issueless:	childless
makeless wife:	wife without a mate
private:	individual
eyes:	images
unthrift:	see sonnets 2, 4 and 6
Shifts but his place:	merely changes the location of wealth
himself:	itself

Sonnet 10
This sonnet takes up the theme of self-hatred mentioned in the couplet of sonnet 9. It depicts the young man's beauty through the image of a house.

unprovident:	reckless (another financial image)
Grant:	I admit
stick'st not:	do not hesitate
roof:	possibly a reference to the young man's position in society as the owner of a great house
fairer lodged:	accommodated in a better place
presence:	exterior
thine:	your child

Sonnet 11
The principal argument here is that if everyone refused to marry, the world would end within a generation. Only unlovely people should die childless.

wane:	diminish, grow old
that which ... departest:	the youth which you are leaving behind
youngly:	as a young man
convertest:	change
Herein:	by this method
minded so:	of this opinion
make ... away:	end the world
store:	parenthood
featureless:	without beauty
Look whom:	whoever
seal:	symbol of beauty
print more:	a seal was used in verifying documents, as evidence of authority or ownership. It could be used again and again

Sonnet 12
This sonnet is pessimistic in tone throughout its first thirteen lines. It uses images of the destruction caused by time, drawn from nature, and expresses no hope until its final line.

brave:	beautiful
past prime:	beyond its prime
sable:	black
erst:	previously
summer's green:	the corn which was green earlier in the summer
girded up:	bound up
borne:	carried
bier:	barrow; litter on which a corpse is carried
go:	die
themselves forsake:	give themselves up
breed:	future generations
brave:	defy (also a reference back to line 2)

Sonnet 13
This sonnet investigates the question of whether the young man is responsible for his own fate. The image of a house occurs again, and the images of husbandry and unthriftiness echo earlier sonnets.

No longer ... live:	master of your fate only while you are alive
this coming end:	your inevitable death
semblance:	appearance
in lease:	on loan
determination:	ending
were:	would be
issue:	child
in honour:	honourably; through marriage
barren:	useless; without children
let ... so:	have a child so that he may call you his father

Sonnet 14
The major image behind this sonnet is of prediction. The poet rejects various methods of prediction, claims that he derives knowledge from the young man's eyes, and predicts either the success of beauty and truth, or the death of both. For comparison, reference should be made to *Love's Labour's Lost*, Act IV, Scene 3, lines 290–340.

methinks:	it seems to me
fortune ... tell:	predict fortunes accurately in great detail
By oft predict that:	by frequent prediction of what
to store:	to parenthood
prognosticate:	predict
end:	death
truth's and ... date:	the death of truth and beauty

Sonnet 15
This is the first sonnet to consider the question of gaining immortality through verse. It includes a complex series of images, many of them from earlier sonnets.

When I consider: a common way of opening a sonnet
holds in perfection: stays perfect
this huge stage: the world (a common Shakespearean image)
influence: power
as: like
Vaunt . . . sap: take pride in their youth
brave state: state of being beautiful
out of memory: beyond the time when anybody remembers
conceit: thought
sullied: dirtied
all in war: in opposition
engraft you: write about you; wish you to have a child

Sonnet 16
This sonnet carries directly on from sonnet 15 (as indicated by the initial 'But') and suggests that art is inferior to nature: the young man will be better preserved through children than through poetry. The sonnet turns upon contrasting images of sterility and life.

tyrant: an image from sonnet 5
barren: unproductive; not bringing forth children
maiden gardens yet unset: virgins as yet without seed
living flowers: this, like the image of the maiden garden, recalls sonnet 15
your painted counterfeit: the description of you in my poetry (an image from drawing)
lines of life: the line from one generation to the next
give away your self: give away your seed
must live: will live
drawn: again an image from drawing

Sonnet 17
Again this sonnet finds that poetry is inferior to life. Poetry is presented as a barren record, and the poet shows his awareness of how near his poetry looks to empty flattery, or unoriginal imitation.

tomb: a very negative image for poetry
fresh numbers: original lines of verse
touches: strokes of art
old men . . . tongue: age is shown here as ugly and untrusted
true rights: true attributes
poet's rage: poet's inspiration
antique song: an old original poem which has been copied

Sonnets 18–32

After the opening group of sonnets the subsequent groupings are more arbitrary and more questionable. The group of sonnets 18–32 includes echoes from earlier sonnets, but there is no further urging of the young man to have children. In general these sonnets are concerned with the patronage of the young man towards the poet, and with the contrast between real and painted beauty.

Sonnet 18

Again the prime of life is depicted through the image of summer, the best time of the year. In contrast to the earlier sonnets, the poet now boasts of the power of his verse to win the young man's immortality.

temperate: even-tempered
summer's lease: the fixed period of summer
eye of heaven: sun
untrimmed: deprived of its trimming
own'st: own, possess
in eternal ... grow'st: you pass from life

Sonnet 19

A sonnet which challenges Time the destroyer. The opening suggests a number of impossible things which Time might attempt; the poet, however, forbids Time to touch the young man's face.

phoenix: a mythological bird said to rise from its own ashes. It could not, therefore, be burned in its own blood
fleet'st: pass quickly
heinous: dreadful
carve not ... pen: this takes up the image of Time's pen from sonnet 16
thy course: the passage of time

Sonnet 20

This sonnet compares the true beauty of the young man with the false beauty of women, whom he resembles. It includes some bawdy innuendo but, more significantly, it is concerned with the difference between constancy and transience, truth and falsehood, throughout.

with nature's ... painted: this implies that the beauty of most women is painted by art not nature
master mistress: he is a man, although he looks like a woman
rolling: moving its attention from object to object
in hue: in complexion
all hues ... controlling: with all colours under his power
steals men's eyes: attracts the attention of men

fell a-doting: become besotted
me of thee defeated: prevented me from possessing you
to my purpose nothing: of no benefit to me
pricked thee out: selected you (a bawdy pun)
thy love's use: your lust

Sonnet 21

This sonnet might be linked with the later group concerned with the Rival Poet. It is concerned with true inspiration and false comparison (a common theme of sonneteers: see also sonnet 130).

that muse: that poet
painted beauty: not the natural beauty of sonnet 20
rehearse: compare
couplement: comparison
in ... hems: contains in this great circle
those gold candles: the stars
hearsay: the exaggeration of rumour, or of unoriginal imitation
purpose: intend
I ... sell: Shakespeare is not writing of his love to offer him for sale; equally, he is denying that he is writing merely to obtain money from his patron

Sonnet 22

In its use of the image of the glass this sonnet is reminiscent of sonnet 3. However, not only does this sonnet develop that image differently, but it also, through a complex conceit, argues that the poet and the young man are one and the same person.

glass: both mirror and, perhaps, the hourglass telling the time
time's furrows: wrinkles on your face
look I: I expect
my ... expiate: should make atonement for my life
seemly raiment: appropriate and beautiful clothing (see sonnet 2)
which: my heart
Bearing thy heart: since I carry our heart
chary: carefully
from faring ill: from becoming ill or, perhaps, from misadventure
Presume ... heart: do not expect your heart to be returned
gave ... again: this reference to gifts again recalls the relationship of patronage

Sonnet 23

This is the first sonnet to use a theatrical image and, like sonnet 21, may refer to the presence of a rival poet seeking the patronage of the young man.

put besides:	made to forget
his part:	his role (perhaps, in this case, the poet's inferiority compared to the young man)
Whose strength:	refers back to 'rage' in line 3
fear of trust:	the poet fears his love is not returned
love's rite:	the ceremony appropriate to love
O'ercharged:	overburdened
burthen:	burden
dumb presagers:	silent prologues. Plays were often preceded by dumb shows, as, for example, in the 'play within a play' in *Hamlet*
that tongue:	possibly the tongue of a rival
more hath more expressed:	has expressed more, more often
belongs to:	is part of

Sonnet 24

This sonnet again questions whether the poet's love is returned, as does sonnet 23. It has an ingenious conceit of a painting within the painter's own body. The final couplet, however, is not totally complimentary, implying either that the artist is not skilled enough to paint the young man's heart, or that the young man is keeping that secret from him.

stelled:	fixed
in table:	on the easel
perspective . . . art:	the painter's art is more evident in his use of perspective
through the painter:	inside the painter
good turns:	favours
wherethrough:	through which
this cunning want:	lack this skill

Sonnet 25

This sonnet deals with the instability of success, including that of patronage, and concludes that the poet is happy because he is secure in the love of his patron.

in favour with their stars:	fortunate. Many people still believe that their fortune is conditioned by planetary movements
bars:	prevents
that I:	what I
but as the marigold . . . eye:	only like the marigold when the sun shines. Marigolds open when the sun shines and close in cloudy weather
a frown:	a frown from the prince
painful warrior:	soldier who endures pain
famousèd:	made famous
foiled:	defeated

razèd:	removed
the rest forgot:	the other victories forgotten
remove:	leave
be removed:	be dislodged

Sonnet 26

This sonnet is explicitly concerned with patronage and the poet's lack of worldly success.

vassalage:	servitude
written ambassage:	that is, his poem
witness:	testify to
bare:	this image of clothing and nakedness is carried through the sonnet (see sonnet 2)
conceit:	opinion
all naked ... it:	will give a home to my bare poem
star:	see sonnet 25
fair aspect:	favourable astrological influence
puts ... loving:	allows one to write more fully (perhaps by giving the poet money)
prove:	test, or, perhaps, reprove

Sonnet 27

This sonnet, and the one which follows it, is concerned with lack of sleep and may link with sonnets 25 and 26, in that all four sonnets may describe the poet's reaction to the young man's absence.

Weary ... haste:	there is an intended paradox in the contrast between these two words
travel:	work
To work:	to tax
Intend:	set out upon
zealous pilgrimage:	a journey of devotion
shadow:	image
ghastly:	ghostly

Sonnet 28

This sonnet develops the image of the opposition between day and night, which occurs frequently in the early sonnets (for example, in sonnet 12). Here, however, day and night join together to torture the poet.

in happy plight:	in good condition
That am:	I who am
in ... hands:	make an agreement
dost him grace:	serve in his stead, shine on his behalf
swart-complexioned:	black-faced
twire not:	do not look out, twinkle
gild'st the even:	makes the evening golden

Sonnet 29

This sonnet deals quite explicitly with the poet's feeling of worldly failure and the consolation brought by his love of the young man. There is little imagery in this sonnet, which makes the simile in line 11 all the more effective.

men's eyes: the opinion of the world
beweep: weep about
outcast state: it is essential for the writer to have a place in society
bootless: useless
Featured: looking, in appearance
scope: intelligence, opportunity
Haply: fortunately, by chance
sullen: dull
sings ... gate: heaven is no longer deaf as it was in line 3

Sonnet 30

This sonnet is similar in theme to sonnet 29. However, it is less concerned with current failure than with remembering past failures.

the sessions: meetings (a legal metaphor)
new wail: bewail once again
drown an eye: drown with tears
dateless: eternal
expense: passing
foregone: gone before
account: a metaphor used extensively in earlier sonnets
fore-bemoanèd moan: complaints which I grieved over before

Sonnet 31

This sonnet, and the one which follows it, returns to the theme of true and false love. In this sonnet the young man is addressed as the total of all the poet's previous loves. The images are predominantly concerned with the Christian burial service.

endeared: made more precious, more beloved
by lacking: by being deprived of them
obsequious tear: tear of mourning
interest of: belonging to
But things removed: merely things absent
trophies: memorials
all ... me: all the parts of me which they had
all they: the sum total of all those former loves

Sonnet 32

This sonnet continues the image of death and burial and returns to the theme of achieving immortality through verse. In this case, however, it is the poet's own immortality which is achieved, through the sincerity of his verse.

my well-contented day: the day of my death, which I look forward to
churl: peasant
bett'ring: improvement (in poetry)
Reserve: continue to read them
vouchsafe: grant
march ... equipage: keep better company

Sonnets 33–42

This somewhat loose group of sonnets seems to be concerned with the separation of the poet and the young man, and the young man's misdemeanour in preferring another to the poet. However, because of the sketchy nature of the narrative, it is not clear whether the fault alluded to in sonnets 33, 34 and 35 is the same as that in sonnet 40.

Sonnet 33
This sonnet seems to develop an image used in sonnet 7: the sun attracting the attention of all the world. The sonnet is not about the poet watching the sun but about the effect of the young man's misdemeanour.

Flatter: stroke, delude
Gilding: making golden
alchemy: magic
rack: wind-driven clouds
fórlorn: saddened, deprived
my sun: the young man
out alack: an expression of dismay
the region cloud: the cloud of the heaven
masked: concealed
no whit: to no extent
stain: be guilty of folly

Sonnet 34
This continues the theme of the previous sonnet. The poet is saddened that the young man has 'sinned' by preferring someone else to him (the 'region cloud' of the previous sonnet). The sonnet continues the image of sun and cloud, developing it into an image of rain.

promise: appear to indicate
base clouds: inferior people (is it the 'Dark Lady' of the later sonnets?)
o'ertake: overtake
bravery: splendour
dry ... face: the young man's attempt to comfort the poet
salve: medicine
give physic to my grief: cure, get rid of, my grief

the strong offence's cross: the pain of the heavy insult
tears are pearl: compare this with *King Lear*, Act IV, Scene 3, lines 21–2
ransom: compensate for

Sonnet 35
This complex sonnet develops the narrative of the previous two sonnets. The poet concludes that he is more culpable than the young man in condoning the young man's fault. The final couplet seems to indicate that the poet's rival is a woman.
loathsome canker: a disease which attacks young plants
Authórizing: justifying
with compare: by the comparison I have made
Myself . . . amiss: corrupting myself in condoning your fault
sense: reason
adverse . . . advocate: the one injured by you is defending you (another legal metaphor)
civil war: war within the poet's self; war conducted politely; war conducted through the court
accessary: an accomplice to a thief
sweet thief which sourly: a paradox (sweet against sour)

Sonnet 36
This sonnet is concerned with the absence of the poet and his friend. It argues that the two will be together though they are apart, their loves being inseparable. It is concerned with the difference in status between the poet and the young man.
twain: two
blots: faults (mentioned in sonnet 35)
borne: tolerated
but one respect: a shared respect
a separable spite: a malicious fate which separates us
sole: unique
my bewailéd guilt: my weeping for my shame
kindness: honour
in such sort: in such a way
report: reputation

Sonnet 37
Again this sonnet is concerned with the poet's inferiority. Here he suggests that his own misfortune is compensated for by the young man's success.
decrepit: physically weak through age
made lame: there is no need to feel that this refers to a real physical deformity on Shakespeare's part

dearest spite:	most severe malice (see sonnet 36)
engrafted:	attached
shadow:	reflection of your worth
sufficed:	satisfied
Look what:	whatever
This ... have:	if I have this wish granted

Sonnet 38

This sonnet, with sonnet 39, is unreserved in its praise of the young man. The two sonnets are linked, but only sonnet 39 brings us back to the principal theme of the group: the unity of their love despite their physical separation.

my muse:	my poetic inspiration
want:	lack
rehearse:	describe
worthy perusal:	worth reading
stand against:	stand in comparison with
light:	guidance
tenth muse:	in classical mythology there were nine muses, divinities presiding over the arts
ten times:	this comparison links with sonnet 37
eternal numbers:	lines of poetry which will never die
slight muse:	feeble poetry
these curious days:	this age when many are pedantic
pain:	labour

Sonnet 39

Like sonnet 36 this sonnet is concerned with the unity between the poet and the young man. It argues that absence is necessary so that the poet will not be praising himself.

with manners:	politely
sour leisure:	unhappy leisure (a paradox with 'sweet leave')
leave:	opportunity
Which:	love
to make ... twain:	to make two people one, or to make one person two

Sonnet 40

The bitterness underlying this sonnet may seem so great a contrast with the previous two sonnets that it may appear to be displaced in the sequence. Although it is obviously linked with sonnet 35, its position here can be justified by its very contrast with sonnet 39. The poet has convinced himself that absence is supportable, and yet, all the time, his friend has been deceiving him with his own mistress. This interpretation is reinforced by sonnet 41.

all my loves: all my mistresses
thou my love receivest: you entertain my mistress
usest: make love with
wilful taste: wilful desire to possess (with a pun on Will)
what thyself refusest: someone whom you do not love
steal thee: steal for yourself
love's wrong...injury: an injury from somebody one loves rather than an attack from an enemy
all ill well shows: all malice appears beautiful
spites: malice

Sonnet 41

The poet understands how the young man can be tempted during his absence. However, in being tempted by the poet's own mistress, the young man is doubly at fault for his own beauty had tempted her to betray the poet.

pretty wrongs: minor faults
liberty: sexual licence
thy years: your youth
assailed: importuned
sourly: in ill-temper
seat: lady
forbear: leave alone
riot: dissolute behaviour
truth: promise (with a pun on 'troth', meaning marital vows)

Sonnet 42

This sonnet cleverly concludes the group by arguing that the poet forgives both the mistress and the young man. It continues the conceit of the poet and the young man being one and the same so that in loving the latter the lady loves the former as well (from sonnets 36 and 39).

hast her: have possessed her
of my wailing chief: my principal grief
suff'ring: allowing
my love's: my mistress's
both twain: both the two of you
lay...cross: torture me in this way
flattery: deception, delusion

Sonnets 43–58

There are pairs of linked sonnets within this group, and extensive use is made of images of eyes and shadows. There is, however, no obvious unity within the group as a whole.

Sonnet 43
This sonnet is concerned with the vision of the young man appearing in a dream. It may imply that the poet is parted from his friend. The images are developed from sonnet 27.

wink:	close my eyes
unrespected:	unimportant
darkly bright:	made bright in the darkness; secretly cheered
shadow:	image
thy shadow's form:	your true self
clearer:	purer
I say:	I repeat
sightless:	closed

Sonnet 44
This sonnet, together with sonnet 45, is concerned with the four elements, earth, water, air and fire. These four are referred to in the context of the young man's absence.

dull substance:	heavy material
As soon as think:	merely by thinking about
so ... wrought:	I am so much made from earth and water
elements so slow:	the two elements of earth and water were thought to make up the duller or slower parts of man
But ... woe:	except heavy tears, symbolic of woe

Sonnet 45
This sonnet continues the image of the elements, concentrating upon the lighter two, air and fire, which are portrayed as running between the poet and his friend.

slight:	insubstantial
desire:	desire is conventionally symbolised as heat
present-absent:	simultaneously present and absent, running between the lovers
slide:	journey
In tender embassy:	as ambassadors of love
of four:	of four elements
life's composition:	the balance of all four elements
straight grow sad:	immediately become sad (because the departure of the lighter two elements has made his body predominantly heavy)

Sonnet 46
This sonnet, together with sonnet 47, portrays a conflict between eye and heart. This sonnet relies upon legal imagery.

mortal war:	war over a living person
Mine eye ... bar:	my eye wishes to deprive my heart of the sight of your picture

never . . . eyes:	not even pierced by eyes made out of crystal
'cide:	decide
title:	legal deed of possession
impanelled:	set up as a jury
quest:	jury
moiety:	share

Sonnet 47

The eye and heart have now agreed their dispute. The principal image in this sonnet is of feasting, an image used in earlier sonnets (see, for example, sonnet 1).

Betwixt:	between
took:	agreed
good turns:	favours
heart . . . smother:	heart smothers himself with sighs because he is in love
my love's picture:	a portrait of my beloved; an image of my emotions
painted banquet:	feast provided by the picture
Thyself away:	while you are absent from me
thy . . . sight:	a reference back to Sonnet 43

Sonnet 48

This sonnet is concerned once again with the separation of the poet from his beloved. The young man is symbolised as a piece of treasure, through the ambiguity of 'dear' (beloved; precious; expensive).

took my way:	went on my journey
trifle:	worthless object
truest:	strongest
unusèd:	unmolested
hands of falsehood:	thieving hands
wards of trust:	trusty guards
worthy . . . grief:	a good example of paradox
dearest:	most beloved; most expensive
chest:	container; heart
at pleasure:	as you wish; for pleasure
proves thievish:	will become a thief

Sonnet 49

This sonnet does not appear to fit into the context of the immediate group. It contains familiar images of being called to account (see sonnets 2 and 4, for example) and of the young man as the sun (sonnet 7, for example). It is, again, based upon legal metaphor.

Against that time:	to protect myself, as insurance, for the time
cast . . . sum:	calculated his final account
audit:	calculation
advised respects:	well thought-out motives

strangely pass:	pass by as if you did not know me
of settled gravity:	from the advice of older people
esconce me here:	defend myself now
my ...uprear:	raise my hand (as if giving evidence)
guard:	protect
laws:	reasonable behaviour
why to love:	why you should love me
allege:	again, a legal metaphor

Sonnet 50

This sonnet returns to the theme of separation between the poet and his friend. It introduces an image which recurs through the next three sonnets: the horse on which the poet rides, which becomes a symbol of his grief.

heavy:	sadly (sadness as a weight runs through this sonnet)
teach:	point out
beast:	horse
dully:	slowly
weight:	weight of my sorrow
wretch:	creature
spur:	the instrument used to goad on horses
provoke him on:	make him move faster
hide:	skin
heavily:	sadly

Sonnet 51

Again the predominant image is that of the slow horse, although reference is made back to the image of swift desire in sonnet 45. Although the poet approved of the horse's slowness when he was going from his beloved, he wants it to run swiftly when he returns.

dull bearer:	slow transport
posting:	hurrying
then:	when I return to you
swift extremity:	all possible speed
wingèd speed:	the speed of wings
shall neigh no dull flesh:	shall not behave like a dull horse (the dullness of the elements as in sonnet 45)
jade:	old horse
wilful slow:	as slowly as I desired
go:	walk

Sonnet 52

This sonnet employs the image of the beloved and precious friend used in sonnet 48. Again the implication is that the poet is separated from his friend.

So am I as:	I am like
For:	for fear of
solemn:	set apart from normal life
captain:	chief
carcanet:	necklace
chest:	treasure-chest; heart (see sonnet 48)
robe:	clothing
Blessèd:	fortunate
scope:	opportunity for me
Being ... hope:	to enjoy your presence, and to anticipate your presence while you are away

Sonnet 53

This sonnet may grow from the other sonnets in this group concerned with substance (sonnets 43, 44 and 45). Its complexity derives from the ambiguity of 'shades' and 'shadow'.

strange shadows ... tend:	images of other people are summed up in you
shade:	shadow
but one:	although you are only one person
lend:	incorporate within you
Adonis:	the classical epitome of male beauty. Shakespeare's first published poem was *Venus and Adonis*
counterfeit:	description
on ... set:	if all the art of beauty were added to Helen's face
Helen:	Helen of Troy, the paragon of female beauty
Grecian tires:	Grecian clothes
foison:	time of plenty, harvest time
bounty:	abundance
you like none:	you are similar to nobody; you do not like anybody

Sonnet 54

This sonnet is very similar to those of the first group (compare, especially, sonnet 5), dwelling upon the folly of dying unwed. It offers the solution of immortality through verse.

beauteous:	beautiful
truth:	lack of artificiality
canker blooms:	wild roses; infected roses
play:	sway
breath:	breeze
maskèd:	hidden
for their virtue only:	because their sole attraction
Die to themselves:	die alone, leaving nothing behind
vade:	fade
truth:	true beauty

Sonnet 55

This is one of the best known sonnets in the sequence. It states that the praise of the young man in the poet's verse will outlast everything else. The paradox is that, in fact, paper is more fragile than any of the substances mentioned in the sonnet.

marble:	the precious stone used for monuments, tombs and statues
gilded:	embellished with decorations
unswept stone:	neglected tombstones
broils:	disputes
masonry:	stone masons
Mars his sword:	the sword of Mars, god of war
oblivious:	uncaring
pace:	step
room:	place (a room rather than tomb)
ending doom:	the day of judgment at the end of the world
that:	when
this:	this verse

Sonnet 56

This sonnet uses again the image of love as a feast, together with one of the most difficult images in the sequence (in lines 9 to 12).

Sweet love:	this could either be a plea to the beloved young man, or to the emotion of love within the poet
edge:	keenness
wink:	are forced to close
perpetual dullness:	permanent indifference
int'rim:	interval
like the ocean ... view:	the difficulty with this image is to decide whether the lovers are divided by the ocean, or whether they come together to the same shore
two contracted new:	two people recently betrothed
As:	or else

Sonnet 57

Another sonnet dealing with separation between poet and young man. The poet characterises himself as a slave in this sonnet.

tend:	wait upon
desire:	pleasures (possibly sexual pleasure)
precious time:	time of my own
services:	occupation
world without end:	interminable
adieu:	farewell
suppose:	imagine
in your will:	a pun on Shakespeare's name

Sonnet 58
This sonnet continues the image of the poet as a slave. The puns in this sonnet blur the distinction between the poet's duty (to accept) and his desire (to restrain the young man).

in thought:	in my mind
at ... crave:	demand from you an account of how you spend your time
vassal:	servant
stay:	await; restrain
beck:	command
of your liberty:	caused by your freedom
suff'rance:	necessity
where you list:	wherever you wish to be
charter:	privilege
privilege your time:	be free with your time
self-doing crime:	crime which injures yourself
to wait:	to act as a servant; to be patient

Sonnets 59–75

This group of sonnets is concerned primarily with the effects of time, not only the destruction caused by time, but also the comparison between the present age and earlier times. This leads into a set of sonnets which are quite critical of the young man's behaviour.

Sonnet 59
This sonnet takes as its theme the familiar saying that there is nothing new under the sun. This leads the poet to look for praise of the young man by earlier writers.

beguiled:	deceived
second ... child:	the second pregnancy of a child already born
composèd:	balanced
revolution:	the revolution of time
wits:	wise men

Sonnet 60
Another sonnet concerned with the destruction caused by time, and with the power of verse. It involves images of the sea, of light, of feeding, and of the scythe.

sequent:	successive
forwards:	in forward motion
Nativity ... light:	the new-born child at first in the ocean of light
Crookèd:	vicious
delves ... brow:	see sonnet 2

rarities ... truth: the most precious parts of nature
but for: except for (see sonnet 12)
times in hope: the future
his cruel hand: the hand of time

Sonnet 61

This sonnet seems to belong to the group dealing with the poet's lack of sleep (sonnets 27, 28 and 43) while separated from the young man.

to: into
mock: tantalise
pry: enquire
wake: wake up

Sonnet 62

This sonnet takes up the conceit of the poet's identification of himself with the young man (used in sonnets 36, 39 and 42).

grounded inward: firmly rooted
glass: mirror (see sonnet 3)
beated and chopped: beaten and creased
antiquity: old age
iniquity: sin
'Tis thee, myself: it is you, my other self
Painting: disguising
days: youth

Sonnet 63

This sonnet continues the now-familiar theme of poetry working against the cruelty of time.

Against: see sonnet 49
o'erworn: worn out
youthful ... night: see sonnet 7
age's: old age's
beauty ... life: the essence of the love will remain although the lover has died
green: fresh, young (contrast between 'black' and 'green')

Sonnet 64

A more pessimistic sonnet than most of those on Time. It does not offer the consolation of immortality through poetry.

fell: foul
razed: destroyed
Increasing ... store: the one gaining at the advantage of the other, thus the latter regaining its territory
state: nation
ruminate: consider
to have: because of

Sonnet 65
This sonnet brings together many of the images used elsewhere in the
sequence to describe the ravages of time.

brass:	see sonnet 64
stone:	see sonnet 55
sea:	see sonnets 60 and 64
with:	against
hold a plea:	make defence (legal metaphor)
action:	legal action
wrackful:	destructive
stout:	strong
time's chest:	the coffin
spoil:	plunder
beauty:	possibly a pun on 'booty', meaning plunder
my love:	my beloved

Sonnet 66
This sonnet is a list of all the reasons the poet might have for leaving the
world: only his love for the young man keeps him going.

these:	the things he is about to list
desert:	deserving
needy nothing:	a worthless person
gilded:	golden
limping sway:	incompetent authority
tongue-tied:	dumb, silent, censored
doctor-like:	like a doctor
simplicity:	naivety

Sonnet 67
This sonnet continues the argument of sonnet 66, wondering why the
young man should continue to live in such a corrupt world.

grace impiety:	sanction sin
lace itself:	adorn itself
dead seeing:	lifeless portrait; mere resemblance
Roses of shadow:	imitation roses
bankrout:	bankrupt
Beggared:	deprived
stores:	treasures
these last:	these recent days

Sonnet 68
Continuing this sequence concerned with the corruptions of the world,
the young man alone remaining untouched, the sole representative of
true beauty. In contrast with earlier sonnets, this sonnet suggests that
beauty need not die: it may be perpetuated dishonestly through
cosmetics.

map:	token
outworn:	gone by
bastard:	artificial, unnatural
borne:	worn
right of sepulchres:	which belong rightly to the grave
a second . . . head:	as wigs
another's green:	the youth of somebody else
store:	cherish
of yore:	in days gone by

Sonnet 69

A bitter sonnet, all the more so after the praise of the previous sonnets. The poet states that, however beautiful the external appearance of the young man might be, the world can see his inner corruption.

Want nothing:	require nothing
give . . . due:	grant you that
even . . . commend:	fairly, without exaggeration
thine own:	what is due to you
confound:	refute
in . . . deeds:	they estimate the worth of this by your behaviour
churls:	impolite fellows
soil:	stain, corruption
common:	ordinary, inferior, undistinguished

Sonnet 70

Having mourned the young man's poor reputation in the previous sonnet the poet finds that it is not surprising: beauty attracts calumny. Many of the images in this sonnet are familiar.

defect:	fault
mark:	target
crow:	a black, ugly bird (in contrast to the lark of sonnet 29)
So thou be good:	if you are truly virtuous
canker vice:	vice as a canker, attacking young plants
prime:	youth
passed . . . days:	avoided the temptations of youth
being charged:	when attacked
tie up envy evermore enlarged:	keep envy captive which will always be abroad; a possible reference to Spenser's *The Faerie Queen* (1593), Book VI, Cant. XII
suspect:	suspicion
owe:	own

Sonnet 71
One of the most affecting sonnets in the sequence. The poet asks the young man not to mourn his death, but to forget him immediately.
surly sullen bell: the bell which tolls to signal a death
vildest: most vile
woe: sorrowful
compounded with: mixed up with
rehearse: repeat
mock you with me: tease you for ever having loved me

Sonnet 72
This sonnet continues the argument of sonnet 71, protesting that there is no virtue in the poet worth praising. It might be ironic, in that many of the charges the poet brings against the young man's false flattery could be made against the sonnets themselves.
recite: catalogue
virtuous lie: lie invented out of the best possible motives
niggard truth: truth that is sparing of praise
untrue: untruthfully
My name: mention of my name
that ... forth: my poetry (Shakespeare is often modest about his verse: see sonnet 76)

Sonnet 73
A very famous sonnet concerned with the poet's age.
yellow leaves: leaves which are yellow with age
Bare ruined choirs: empty ruined churches
Death's second self: the comparison of death and sleep is common in Shakespeare: see, for example, *Hamlet*, Act 3, Scene 1
ashes of his youth: the ashes of youthful desire (see sonnet 45)
consumed ... by: compare sonnet 1
which ... long: because the poet will die

Sonnet 74
This sonnet carries on from sonnet 73 (indicated by the 'But'). The sonnet distinguishes between the body, which is worthless, and inner worth.
fell: foul
arrest ... bail: a metaphor from capture
interest: portion
reviewest: read over
spirit: soul
dregs: worthless left-overs
wretch: death or time
this: this poem

Sonnet 75

The concluding sonnet of this group catalogues the conflict of emotions within the poet: it is based upon a series of paradoxes.

for the peace ... strife:	for the peace I find through you I am faced with such trouble
anon:	immediately
filching:	stealing
bettered:	convinced that it is better
clean:	entirely
pine and surfeit:	starve and feast
Or:	either

Sonnets 76–96

The principal idea in this group of sonnets is the poet's jealousy of a rival poet. Thus, this group continues the preoccupation with poetry initiated in sonnet 72 and sonnet 74. The group also deals with the poet's unworthiness and the young man's low opinion of him.

Sonnet 76

This sonnet encapsulates the feelings of Elizabethan poets about the use of convention. The final couplet sums up what Shakespeare is attempting to achieve: to describe afresh an age-old emotion.

barren:	empty
pride:	ornament
with ... methods:	this implies that there were contemporary poets prepared to deviate from the tradition
compounds:	mixture of style
noted weed:	familiar manner
where ... proceed:	who was their author
all my best:	my best effort
my love:	my pleasure

Sonnet 77

The poet urges the young man to write a book of his own, in order to conquer age and Time. The sonnet is tightly structured, referring to the glass, the sundial, and the book in turn.

glass:	mirror
dial:	sundial, a mode of telling the time
vacant leaves:	empty pages of a book
mouthèd:	gaping, empty
shady stealth:	evil progress (a sundial works by throwing a shadow)
thievish progress:	progress by stealing from life
Look what:	whatever

waste blanks: empty pages
Those children nursed: when you have set down these ideas
offices: practices (looking in the mirror, at the sundial, at the book)

Sonnet 78
This is the first sonnet explicitly referring to the rival poet. It is linked with the previous sonnet in that the success of the poet's description of the young man has led to his becoming a tradition in his own right.
invoked: called upon for inspiration
muse: see sonnet 38
alien pen: other poet
use: practice, habit
the learned's wing: the inspiration of wise men
but mend the style: become a mere ornament
And ... be: and what was already sophisticated is increased by your presence
my ... ignorance: compare sonnet 72 for this modesty about his own verse

Sonnet 79
This sonnet develops the argument of sonnet 78. On the one hand the poet seems to understand why the young man is praised by others; on the other hand he accuses these poets of robbery.
Whilst ... aid: when I was the only poet seeking inspiration from you
gracious numbers: beautiful verses
sick muse: weak, inferior poetry
give ... place: acknowledge the superiority of another
thy ... argument: the description of your beauty
travail: labour

Sonnet 80
The poet now begs to be allowed to continue to write, even though acknowledging his inferiority to his rival. The principal image is of ships sailing on the ocean.
might: energy
To make: which makes
The humble ... bear: can tolerate my humble praise in addition to his superior poetry
saucy bark: small boat
main: sea
wilfully: a pun on the poet's name
soundless deep: bottomless ocean
wracked: wrecked
of ... building: of elaborate design

Sonnet 81
This sonnet appears almost to be misplaced, since it makes no reference to the rival poet. However, it is linked with sonnet 82 and that sonnet is clearly tied in with the rest of the series.

Or:	either
epitaph to make:	to write a verse in your memory
in ... rotten:	am dead and buried
From hence:	from this moment
o'er-read:	read over
tongues to be:	people not yet born
rehearse:	repeat
this world:	this present generation
virtue:	power

Sonnet 82
Again, the poet charges his rival with insincerity. The poet claims plainness and natural description (similar images are used to those in sonnet 68).

grant:	confess
muse:	poetry
attaint:	blame
hue:	external appearance
limit:	target
time-bett'ring:	improving
strainèd touches:	forced writing
sympathized:	summed up in a life-like manner
true plain words:	compare *Love's Labour's Lost*, Act 5, Scene 2
Where cheeks need blood:	where inferior beauty needs the praise to make it appear more beautiful

Sonnet 83
This sonnet continues the argument of sonnet 82, claiming that the poet has deliberately paid little attention to the description of the young man's appearance, concentrating instead on his true worth. Those who praise his beauty do it a disservice.

painting:	exaggerated praise
fair:	fairness, beauty
barren tender:	feeble effort
have I slept ... report:	I have neglected to praise you
extant:	alive
quill:	pen
of worth:	worthily
impute:	charge
bring a tomb:	write in a dull and deadening manner
both your poets:	Shakespeare and the rival poet

Sonnet 84
This sonnet deals with the complex question of how the young man should be praised and whether he is not, in himself, a true poem. The implication, however, is that he is too susceptible to flattery.

you alone are you:	you are unique
store:	source of beauty
example:	give an example of
penury:	poverty
so:	thereby
counterpart:	copy
style:	pen; writing
fond on:	foolishly flattered by

Sonnet 85
This sonnet is similar in theme to sonnet 23, dealing with the poet's reticence. Like the earlier sonnet, this sonnet argues that silence can sometimes be more meaningful than words.

in manners:	politely
holds . . . still:	keeps silent
Reserve:	preserve
filed:	recorded; polished
unlettered clerk:	an inferior member of the church
cry . . . hymn:	an image from the Christian religious service
hindmost:	last
holds . . . before:	is first in rank
Then . . . respect:	then, although you may respect others for what they say
in effect:	in truth

Sonnet 86
This sonnet investigates the reason for the poet's silence. It employs images from earlier sonnets.

proud full sail:	see sonnet 80
Bound:	journeying
inhearse:	bury
spirit:	inspiration (see sonnet 85)
spirits:	immortal beings
compeers:	allies
astonishèd:	frightened away
gulls:	deceives
filled up his line:	appeared in his poetry
matter:	subject matter

Sonnet 87
This sonnet marks the poet's acknowledgement of the inevitability of his losing the young man.

for my possessing: for me to own
like enough: probably
charter ... worth: privilege of being worthy
bonds: claims
determinate: at an end
thy granting: your permission
patent: right to have you
mistaking: wrongly valuing
misprision: deception, misconception
Comes ... again: returns back to you again
on ... making: when you have made a more considered judgement
In ... king: dreaming I was a king

Sonnet 88

This sonnet, like many others, deals with a hypothetical future event: in this case the young man failing to value the poet. It makes substantial use of legal metaphors.

disposed to: inclined to
set ... light: have a low opinion of me
in the eye : in the centre
art forsworn: have broken your word
With ... acquainted: since I know my own weakness best
part: behalf
set ... story: give evidence
attainted: accused
For bending: because, in inclining
to thee ... belong: the unity of poet and young man is frequently asserted in the sequence
thy right: your cause

Sonnet 89

This sonnet continues the theme of the previous sonnet: the poet defining the extent of his own unworthiness. The sonnet is an ingenious conceit: if the young man dislikes him the poet must hate himself.

Say that: if
comment upon: add to your description of
halt: hobble
love: my beloved
To set ... change: to make it clear that our relationship has changed
will: desire (with a pun on Will)
acquaintance strangle: stop being acquainted with you
look strange: appear as a stranger
Lest I: for fear that I
haply: perhaps
vow debate: promise to dispute

Sonnet 90
This sonnet continues the concern with the young man's poor opinion of the poet, arguing that, since the poet's fortune is generally at a low ebb, it is appropriate that now should be the time for the young man to turn against him.

if ever, now:	if you are to do it at any time, do it now
bent:	determined
bow:	buckle
after-loss:	afterthought
'scaped:	escaped
in the rearward of:	behind
linger out:	prolong
done:	completed
strains:	parts, causes, kinds

Sonnet 91
This sonnet begins in a much more optimistic vein than its immediate predecessors. However, it is clear that this optimism is more apparent than real, because the first couplet is one of despair at the loss of the young man's favour.

their birth:	the rank they hold by birth
force:	strength
new-fangled:	fashionably new
humour:	whim
adjunct:	attendant, accompanying
one general best:	a single, general superiority
pride:	wealth, pleasure

Sonnet 92
This sonnet argues that the poet's life will end with the young man's displeasure. It builds to a climax, that death is to be welcomed, only to conclude that the poet may be unaware of the young man's falseness.

steal thyself away:	take yourself from me
term of life:	my lifetime
assurèd:	certainly
life:	my life
a better state:	the life after death, salvation
my life ... lie:	my life will end when you are unfaithful
title:	entitlement, fate
but ... blot:	see sonnet 70

Sonnet 93
This sonnet develops the final couplet of sonnet 92, giving reasons why the poet, deceived by the young man's charm and good looks, might be unaware of any infidelity on the young man's part.

in that:	from your eye
history:	story
writ:	written
in thy creation:	when you were born
How ... show:	a bitter couplet, suggesting that the beauty of the young man could be as deceptive as that of the apple which deceived Eve in *Genesis*, 3:6
answer not thy show:	does not correspond to your appearance

Sonnet 94

There has been more written about this sonnet than about any other—an indication both of its richness and its difficulty. It appears to continue the theme of sonnet 93: the ease with which the young man can conceal his emotions. The difficulty is whether we are to consider this ability as a positive attribute or not. Another is the relationship of octave and sestet.

They that ... do none:	as has been often pointed out, the opening line contains an irony, giving first an impression of something negative, and abruptly changing to a positive image
do show:	appear to be going to do
rightly:	justly
husband:	look after
expense:	waste
lords and owners:	in control
to ... sweet:	part of the general sweetness of summer
to itself:	in itself
outbraves:	exceeds
Lilies:	beautiful flowers
fester:	rot

Sonnet 95

This sonnet develops the notion from the previous sonnet that the young man's beautiful appearance hides an inner vice. Like sonnet 94 it has a final line which could stand on its own as a proverb.

canker:	see sonnet 35
budding name:	reputation which is in the process of being formed
sweets:	delights
lascivious comments:	coarse rumours
sport:	sexual misbehaviour
habitation:	dwelling
edge:	sharpness

Sonnet 96

The final sonnet of this group also deals with the young man's fault and the way it is forgiven because of his beauty. It has the same final couplet as sonnet 36, a fact which has caused some editors to feel that it does not belong here and to explain its presence as printer's error. Yet the couplet seems to fit in with the rest of the poem satisfactorily.

Some say . . . sport:	the opening two lines point to the fact that the young man's behaviour might be censured or condoned
resort:	flock
deemed:	judged
translate:	change
lead away:	deceive
state:	power
But . . . report:	this couplet makes sense as a plea for the young man not to use his power for fear of ruining the poet's reputation

---

Sonnets 97–108

This group of sonnets seems to be separated from the group which precedes it. They are concerned with the absence of the poet from his friend.

Sonnet 97

The poet has been separated from his friend for the seasons of summer and winter. However, the pain of separation has made these seasons seem like winter.

the pleasure . . . year:	you who are the pleasure of my old age
bareness:	absence of leaves from the trees
teeming:	fertile
big:	pregnant
wanton burthen of the prime:	varied fruit of spring
wait on thee:	are your servants; wait for your return
thou . . . mute:	this idea of the natural world mirroring human emotion is frequent in poetry. It is known as the 'pathetic fallacy'
dull a cheer:	sad a mood

Sonnet 98

This sonnet continues the conceit that the absence has seemed like winter, although the season was spring. This time the weather does not correspond with the poet's mood but, in contrast, mocks him with its cheerfulness.

proud-pied:	beautifully varied
trim:	finery
heavy Saturn:	Saturn was thought to cause melancholy
lays:	song
summer's story:	happy tale
pluck them:	pluck the flowers
vermilion:	red
shadow:	image

Sonnet 99

This fifteen-line sonnet continues the idea of sonnet 98: that the beauties of spring are a copy of his friend's beauty.

forward:	early
chide:	reproach
annexed thy breath:	captured your breath (as its perfume)
canker:	see sonnet 35
But:	except

Sonnet 100

This sonnet implies that, during his absence, the poet has written no verse on the subject of the young man.

muse:	inspiration
might:	power
fury:	see sonnet 17 for a similar image of inspiration
Dark'ning:	using up
redeem:	make up for
numbers:	verses
lays:	songs
resty:	lazy
a satire to:	an attacker of
time's spoils:	the attacks of time
his scythe:	the scythe of time (see sonnet 60)

Sonnet 101

The poet looks for reasons why he has not written about the young man for so long. It is similar in theme, tone, and imagery to sonnet 85.

truant:	absent for no cause
amends:	recompense
my love:	the young man
haply:	perhaps
lay :	describe
't lies in thee:	it lies in your power
outlive ... tomb:	see sonnet 55
ages yet to be:	see sonnet 81
thy office:	your duty
long hence:	for far distant ages

Sonnet 102

This sonnet continues the theme of the sincerity of the poet's love, despite his silence. He uses images from sonnet 21 and argues, in addition, that praise of his friend is now so common that he has ceased to write because his voice would be unheard.

in seeming:	in external appearance
merchandised:	advertised as for sale (see sonnet 21)
esteeming:	estimated worth
publish:	make known
wont:	accustomed
greet:	celebrate
lays :	songs
Philomel:	the poetic name for the nightingale
in summer's front:	as herald to summer, at the beginning of summer
her pipe:	her singing
wild music:	the music of nature
sweets grown common:	beautiful things which have become common
her:	the nightingale
dull:	make you sated

Sonnet 103

This sonnet returns to the familiar theme that the young man is himself a poem and needs no further praise.

Alack:	alas
a scope:	an opportunity
pride:	beauty
argument:	the subject, the young man himself
beside:	in addition
overgoes:	outdoes
blunt:	unsophisticated, plain
quite:	entirely
striving to mend:	in trying to improve
To ... well:	to ruin the subject that was perfect before
pass:	subject, purpose

Sonnet 104

This sonnet tells us that the relationship between poet and patron has lasted three years. It argues that, although no change is obvious in the young man's beauty, some change must have taken place.

eyed:	saw
pride:	beauty
green:	young
dial hand:	the hand of a sundial which moves imperceptibly
steal ... figure:	move away from its number (on the dial)
unbred:	unborn

Sonnet 105
The poet pleads that his love shall not be regarded as idolatry even though his poems are all on the same theme. Since his friend is constant, his verse must also be constant. It is similar to sonnet 76.

as an idol show: appear to be an idol
To one, of one: dedicated to one person, about one person
difference: other themes; disputes
change: the alteration between fair, true, and kind
scope: opportunity, range
kept seat: dwelt together

Sonnet 106
This sonnet is concerned with the conventions of earlier poetry. It may be linked with sonnet 59.

chronicle: history
wasted time: time gone by
wights: people (a consciously archaic word to recall ages gone by)
blazon: conventional catalogue of the beauties of a lady
antique: old
prefiguring: predicting
for: although
divining eyes: eyes of prediction
wonder: marvel

Sonnet 107
This sonnet is based on familiar themes of man's mortality and the inevitability of all things coming to an end.

lease: prescribed date
supposed as forfeit: believed to be subject
confined doom: particular fate
The mortal ... endured: believed by some editors to be a reference to the English defeat of the Spanish Armada in 1588
presage: prediction
olives: symbol of peace
balmy: healthy
subscribes: defers
tyrants' crests ... spent: reminiscent of sonnet 55

Sonnet 108
This sonnet argues that every aspect of his love for the young man has been dealt with by the poet.

character: describe
figured: written
thou mine, I thine: you are mine, I yours
hallowed: made holy (a reference back to the 'prayers' of line 5)

case:	appearance
for aye his page:	forever his servant (sonnet 107 proved time deferring to the poet)
conceit:	thought

Sonnets 109–126

This is the last group of sonnets to deal with the relationship between the poet and the young man.

Sonnet 109
This sonnet is concerned with the poet's absence from the young man and argues that this absence is not equivalent to infidelity.

false of heart:	unfaithful
flame:	love
qualify:	reduce
breast:	heart
ranged:	travelled
Just:	punctual
exchanged:	changed
myself . . . stain:	through the tears of the poet
blood:	flesh

Sonnet 110
This sonnet argues that the poet's absence has enabled him, by experiencing false friendship, to appreciate fully the young man's love.

motley:	jester, fool
Gored:	injured; dirtied
old offences:	familiar crimes
Most true it is:	this phrase may be an echo of Sidney's *Astrophil and Stella*, sonnet 5
Askance:	sideways, falsely
blenches:	stains
another youth:	a fresh vitality
essays:	trials
grind:	sharpen (anticipating sonnet 118)
try:	test, evaluate
next . . . best:	the best love after the love of heaven

Sonnet 111
This sonnet is concerned with the poet's lack of wordly success. It appears to refer to his difficulty in having to serve public taste in the theatre in order to earn his living, and appeals to his friend for sympathy. It includes a complex set of images.

chide:	dispute
public manners:	vulgar behaviour
brand:	stain
subdued:	reduced
dyer's hand:	the dyer's hand becomes stained with the dye itself
eisel ... infection:	vinegar in order to cure my disease

Sonnet 112

It may be that this sonnet continues to deal with the poet's career as dramatist. Here he seems to be willing to accept criticism from nobody except the young man.

impression:	the hollow made by the stamp of scandal
o'ergreen:	cover over
None also ... wrong:	these obscure lines may well be corrupt
adder's sense:	adders were thought to be deaf
That ... dead:	that you appear to be the only alive thing in the world

Sonnet 113

After one sonnet which referred to deafness, this sonnet refers to the poet's partial blindness: his inability to perceive the world properly.

is in my mind:	looks inwardly
Doth part:	performs part of
out:	blind
latch:	see
rud'st:	most rude
sweet favor:	beautifully proportioned
the crow, or dove:	for a similar contrast see sonnet 70
replete:	satisfied completely
untrue:	false; blind

Sonnet 114

This sonnet continues the image of the poet's sight being affected by the young man. It is concerned with objects seeming more lovely than they really are, and the dangers of flattery.

Or whether:	this opening makes it clear that this sonnet follows directly on from sonnet 113
Drink up:	note the recurrent image of flattery as a drink
alchemy:	magic
indigest:	without form
cherubins:	angels
to ... assemble:	come within the range of my eye
most kingly:	like a king
gust:	taste
greeing:	agreeing

Sonnet 115
This sonnet is again concerned with the passage of time. The claim here, however, is that the poet's love for the young man is not static but a growing form which will improve.

My . . . flame: my strongest flame of love
'twixt vows: to alter promises
Tan . . . beauty: make beauty itself deteriorate
alt'ring: diverting
Crowning the present: assuming that the present time is the best

Sonnet 116
This famous sonnet is concerned with need for love to match the changes of time: in this respect it carries on the theme of sonnet 115. It is based upon the wording of the Christian marriage service in the *Book of Common Prayer*.

impediments: obstacles
alters: ceases
Or . . . remove: or ends when one party goes away
ever-fixèd: permanent
looks on: faces
bark: ship
time's fool: subject to time
bending sickle: the shape of the scythe; the changeability of time ('bend' as in line 4)
compass: range
bears it out: lasts, endures
edge of doom: end of the world

Sonnet 117
This sonnet deals with the ways in which the poet has wasted his time during his absence from the young man. It argues that all of this was merely to test his love.

scanted: given grudgingly
unknown minds: worthless people
your . . . right: what is due to you
hoisted . . . winds: been promiscuous
Book: record
surmise accumulate: add suspicion
level: range

Sonnet 118
This sonnet argues that it is necessary to sharpen the poet's love for the young man by meeting inferior people. It develops an image used in sonnet 110 and makes use also of images drawn from contemporary medical practices.

eager compounds: acidic sauces
sicken: made ourselves ill by using an emetic
sick of: tired of
meetness: aptness
policy: strategy
faults assured: real errors

Sonnet 119

This sonnet develops the medical imagery used in sonnet 118, listing the potions taken by the poet to cure himself of his love of the young man.

siren tears: falsely alluring tears
limbecks: alembics, apparatus used for distilling
Whilst . . . never: whilst it deluded itself that it had never been happier
fitted: in fits of madness

Sonnet 120

This sonnet is concerned with the unkindness inflicted by the two friends on each other. It appears to record the outcome of a quarrel between them.

befriends: comforts, reassures
my transgressions: my sin of being unkind to you
nerves: sense of feeling
night of woe: worst time of sorrow
rememb'red: reminded
But that: except that

Sonnet 121

A sonnet concerned with the differences between being sinful and having a reputation for sinning. It questions whether others are in a position to censure him, since they may be guilty of sin themselves.

vile esteemed: reputed evil
not . . . being: not being evil I nevertheless have the reputation of being so
just: innocent
adulterate: deceived
Give salvation: act upon
wills: opinions
level: accuse
straight: innocent
be bevel: bend (with the weight of sin)
By: by comparison with
rank: evil

Sonnet 122

The principal image in this sonnet is of the memorandum, the book in which the poet records his memories of his love.

tables:	memoranda
charactered:	described
idle rank:	useless book
razed:	destroyed
missed:	lost
That . . . retention:	these poor books
these . . . more:	that is, the mind; the heart
adjunct:	another way
import:	impute

Sonnet 123

This sonnet is again concerned with the power of love to defeat time. It may refer to some newly discovered ancient monument which has given information about times gone by.

novel:	new
dressings:	symbols
dates:	lifetimes
foist:	thrust
make:	believe
registers:	monuments
thee:	time
doth lie:	is not a true and stable thing
scythe:	see sonnet 60 and sonnet 12

Sonnet 124

This sonnet continues the comparison between love and a building, relating other images of impermanence to that more permanent entity.

love:	feeling of love
child of state:	product of chance
for . . . unfathered:	be disowned as worthless offspring of fortune
As:	either
suffers . . . in:	does not endure
thrallèd discontent:	political upheaval
inviting:	beckoning, alluring
policy:	intrigue, self-interest
works on:	influences
all alone:	unsupported
largely politic:	immensely wise
Which . . . crime:	who, having lived wickedly, justly perish

Sonnet 125

The poet rejects the false charge of trying without success to gain patronage. He spoke the truth without looking for reward.

Were't aught:	would it matter
bore . . . canopy:	carried the canopy (showed my service to one of superior rank)
extern:	outward show
dwellers . . . favor:	these who flatter in hope of gain
paying . . . rent:	flattering too much
compound sweet:	elaborate, artificial compliment
simple savor:	unadorned truth
oblation:	praise
mixed . . . seconds:	tempered by flattery
render:	surrender
suborned informer:	false accuser
impeached:	accused
least . . . control:	least in the power of falsehood

Sonnet 126

The sonnets to the young man are brought to a close with this twelve-line poem. It warns the young man to take the approach of death seriously, even though he still appears young. In imagery it is very similar to sonnet 3.

glass:	mirror; hourglass
hour:	hourglass
grown:	improved
wrack:	destruction
still . . . back:	always keeps you young
to this purpose:	for this purpose
minutes:	passage of time
minion:	servant
audit:	final account
quietus:	final statement

Sonnets 127–154

The remaining sonnets are concerned with the poet's love for a dark-haired lady. In contrast with his love for the young man, this passion irritates the poet for he does not respect the lady and often expresses his self-disgust at having fallen in love with her. Many of the incidents touched upon in earlier groups are re-examined from a new perspective.

Sonnet 127

This sonnet establishes that the sonnets to the lady are not to be conventionally complimentary. It takes the conventional image of the beautiful, fair-haired lady and inverts it, ingeniously explaining why his lady is dark. A similar argument is made in *Love's Labour's Lost*, Act 4, Scene 3, ll. 254—61.

old age: earlier times
counted: considered
fair: beautiful (with a contrast between 'black' and 'fair')
beauty's successive heir: the legitimate child of beauty
For ... face: for since it became the practice to use cosmetics to do the work of nature
bow'r: dwelling place
suited: matching
esteem: appearance
becoming ... woe: looking like mourners

Sonnet 128
This sonnet is built around an incident: the lady playing a musical instrument (a spinet or virginal). The poet envies the good fortune of the keys of the instrument which are touched by the lady.

my music: the poet calls the young man 'music' in sonnet 8
wood: instrument
sway'st: controls
wiry concord: harmony of the strings
confounds: overpowers
jacks: keys (with a pun on 'men')
harvest: reward
they: my lips
gait: pace
saucy: impertinent keys; lascivious men

Sonnet 129
This sonnet expresses a profound sense of disgust at the whole business of courtship. Conventionally, love was supposed to ennoble the lover: to lead to ultimate salvation. In contrast it leads here, through frustration and degradation, to hell.

Th'expense ... action: lust is, in effect, the expenditure of life in unprofitable shame
till action: until the consummation of lust
straight: immediately
Past reason: unreasonably
as ... bait: in the way a lure would be hated by a fish
laid: set
so: that is, mad
extreme: intemperate
A ... proof: a pleasure for the moment of action
proposed: anticipated
behind, a dream: afterwards, a mere illusion
heav'n: the physical delight

Sonnet 130

This sonnet takes the conventional blazon (see sonnet 106) and inverts it, challenging all the usual comparisons between the lady's appearance and naturally beautiful phenomena.

dun:	grey
damasked:	dappled (see sonnet 99)
reeks:	a very unpoetic and unflattering verb
go:	walk
by heaven:	an oath, but also recalling the goddess of the previous line
rare:	beautiful
belied:	mispraised
compare:	comparison

Sonnet 131

This sonnet develops the symbolism of the lady's blackness. Its tone is primarily ironic and humorous, suggesting that, although others may suggest that the lady is not very beautiful, the poet secretly denies this. Her behaviour, however, may be reprehensible.

so as thou art:	even looking as you do
that:	who
I ... bold:	I am too polite
one ... neck:	one after the other

Sonnet 132

In this sonnet the blackness of the lady's eyes is explained as being caused by her mourning for the pain of the poet.

ruth:	pity
morning:	pun on 'mourning'
becomes:	is suited
beseem:	match with
doth ... grace:	makes you appear attractive
foul:	ugly

Sonnet 133

The lady has been unfaithful with the poet's friend. Thus this sonnet deals with the same subject as sonnets 40, 41 and 42 but from a new perspective.

Beshrew:	curse
slave ... slavery:	subject to your slavery
my next self:	my second self (the young man)
engrossed:	ensnared
Prison:	imprison
bail:	release
guard:	prison
pent:	imprisoned

Sonnet 134

This sonnet continues the theme of the previous sonnet, using predominantly legal and financial imagery to describe the relationship between poet, mistress, and young man.

mortgaged:	promised, offered as security
will:	desire
so that:	if
surety-like . . . me:	to woo you on my behalf
bond:	bargain
statute:	security
take:	use up
usurer . . . use:	usurer who lends all her wealth
sue:	enslave

Sonnet 135

This sonnet, and the one which follows it, puns on the name Will, which may be the name of the young man as well as of the poet. 'Will' can also mean 'desire', as well as having a bawdy reference to the male sexual organ.

to boot:	in addition
vouchsafe:	agree
The . . . still:	although the sea is composed entirely of water, it receives water from the rain
no unkind:	no unkind persons
fair beseechers:	flatterers
kill:	kill your desire for me

Sonnet 136

check thee that:	reprimand you because
Thus far:	to that extent
sweet:	sweet lady
things . . . receipt:	important matters
a number . . . none:	a single thing is discounted
untold:	unnoticed

Sonnet 137

This sonnet is addressed to love's blindness, and asks why the poet should be deceived into loving a lady he knows to be neither beautiful in appearance nor faithful in deeds.

blind fool:	Cupid, the symbol of love, was a blind boy
behold . . . see:	compare sonnets 113 and 114
lies:	is; deceives; sleeps
over-partial:	prejudiced, biased
several plot:	a private place
common:	promiscuous
put upon:	attribute

Sonnet 138

This sonnet investigates the reasons why truth might sometimes need to be suppressed. It is based upon the various senses of 'lie' (developing from line 3 of sonnet 137).

made:	a pun on 'maid'
lies:	tells me a lie; sleeps with others
That:	I believe her so that
Simply:	foolishly
credit:	believe
simple:	plain
told:	counted

Sonnet 139

The poet calls upon the lady to confess her infidelity and not to wound him by looking elsewhere.

with pow'r:	openly
forbear:	refrain
o'erpressed:	conquered
my love:	my lady
my foes:	her glances
with looks:	by looking at me
rid:	get rid of

Sonnet 140

This sonnet involves the conceit that the poet, if treated too disdainfully by the lady, might go mad and speak ill of her in his fury.

press:	injure
pity-wanting pain:	my pain which is worthy of pity
wit:	skill, intelligence
testy:	irritable
ill-wresting:	ill-believing
belied:	slandered, lied about
Bear . . . straight:	look at nobody else

Sonnet 141

This sonnet is, again, far from conventional, in that the poet lists the lady's defects, and the reasons why he does not love her. Nevertheless, he is in her power, and relieved that he is punished by her for the sin of loving her.

errors:	blemishes; sins
of view:	of what I can see
unswayed:	out of control
vassal wretch:	miserable slave
plague . . . gain:	a paradox
awards . . . pain:	punishes me for that sin

Sonnet 142
This sonnet develops the theme of the poet's sin, and asks the lady to compare her own sin with his.

grounded on:	based upon
merits not reproving:	does not deserve to be punished
profaned ... ornaments:	(you have) misused the beauty of your lips
Robbed ... rents:	made husbands be unfaithful to their wives
importune:	persuade passionately

Sonnet 143
This sonnet is built upon an extended simile comparing the poet to a baby left by its mother while she runs after an escaped chicken.

Lo:	a poetic word of introduction
swift despatch:	speed
stay:	stay where it is
holds ... chase:	runs after her
bent:	concentrated
will:	a pun on the poet's name

Sonnet 144
This famous sonnet compares the poet's love for the young man with that for the Dark Lady. It is linked with sonnets 133 and 134, which dealt with the liaison between the young man and the Dark Lady. The comparison of the two loved ones to Good and Bad angels tempting the soul of the poet is derived from medieval drama.

of ... despair:	one of which comforts me, the other drives me to despair
suggest:	talk to
right fair:	truly beautiful; truly just
pride:	lust
in ... hell:	a reference to the possible copulation of the young man and the lady
fire ... out:	pass on disease to my good angel

Sonnet 145
This sonnet appears quite conventional, dealing with an incident in which the lady is apparently vowing her hatred of the poet, only for the poet to hear a different message in the final line. However, line 13 may include a veiled allusion to Shakespeare's own wife, Anne Hathaway.

love's:	Cupid's
languished:	pined
straight:	immediately
doom:	judgement
I hate ... you:	she changed her words from those of hatred by saying 'I hate not you'

Sonnet 146
The text of this sonnet is corrupt, in that the first two lines include confusing repetition. The theme of the sonnet is the distinction between the soul and the body, and the way in which the one may profit as the other decays.

thy ... walls:	the body
cost:	expenditure
lease:	lifetime
fading mansion:	the body which is subject to decay
live thou:	may you improve
let that pine:	let the body decay
terms divine:	timeless salvation

Sonnet 147
This sonnet is based upon an extended comparison between love and a disease, including reference to medicines and doctors.

still:	always
preserve:	prolong
prescriptions ... kept:	advice is not followed
approve:	discover that
physic did except:	medicine kept away
evermore:	continual
At random:	far

Sonnet 148
This sonnet appears to belong with sonnets 113, 114 and 137, all of which are concerned with the poet's failure to see things properly.

censures:	criticises
vexed:	troubled, afflicted
watching:	staying awake
mistake my view:	do not see correctly

Sonnet 149
This sonnet develops the theme of the poet's blindness. He wonders that the lady can be so cruel to him, when he so obviously worships her, and concludes that it is this very doting that she despises.

cruel:	cruel lady
partake:	take sides
I ... myself:	I neglect to take care of myself
fawn upon:	admire uncritically
lour'st:	frown
all my best:	all my talents
those ... lov'st:	you love only those who see things clearly

Sonnet 150
Again the poet asks what power the lady has to make him love against all he knows or sees.

from what pow'r:	from what mighty god
With ... sway:	to rule my heart even though you are unworthy
becoming ... ill:	talent to make bad things appear good
refuse:	dross
abhor my state:	despise my wretched fortune

Sonnet 151
This sonnet is full of bawdy innuendo about the physical effects that the poet's desire for the lady has upon him.

Love ... young:	a reference to the boy Cupid, symbol of love
urge ... amiss:	do not emphasise my sin
stays:	waits for
rising:	a bawdy allusion
fall ... side:	fight on your behalf (with a further bawdy pun)

Sonnet 152
This sonnet refers to the promises that have been broken by the poet and the Dark Lady in their adulterous relationship.

am forsworn:	have broken my oath
to:	in
In act ... bearing:	you have broken your marriage-vow in the act of love with me, and have broken that new vow by now swearing hatred of me
misuse:	describe falsely
of:	about
enlighten:	make seem more fair
eye:	a pun on 'I'

Sonnet 153
The final two sonnets have little connection with the rest of the sequence. They are conventional sonnets in praise of the mistress, complimenting her by involving her in a story based upon the classical figures of Cupid and Diana.

laid by:	put aside
brand:	torch
A maid of Dian's:	a servant of the virgin goddess Diana. Disputes between Diana and Cupid are common in classical legend
borrowed:	received
dateless:	undying
needs would:	must
hied:	went
distempered:	unwell

Sonnet 154
This sonnet extends the narrative begun in sonnet 153 and concludes with an epigrammatic final line.

The ... god:	Cupid
votary:	worshipper
general:	leader
by:	nearby

Part 3

Commentary

Known facts

W.H. Auden* writes of Shakespeare's sonnets that the certain facts are just two in number:

> Two of the sonnets, 'When my love swears that she is made of truth' (138), and 'Two loves I have, of comfort and despair' (144) appeared in *The Passionate Pilgrim*, a poetic miscellany printed in 1599, and the whole collection was published by G. Eld for T.T. in 1609 with a dedication 'To The Onlie Begetter Of These Insuing Sonnets. Mr W.H.'

The first edition of 1609 is generally believed to have been registered by Thomas Thorpe and its authenticity has repeatedly been challenged. Some critics have questioned the ordering of this edition, others Shakespeare's authorship of certain of the sonnets. The first of these challenges will be discussed later, the second may be rejected entirely. A second edition of the sonnets was published in 1640 with an ordering different from the 1609 edition, but few critics have found this edition authoritative.

A great deal of attention has been paid to the title page and dedication of the 1609 edition. There has been much dispute as to the meaning of the phrase 'The Onlie Begetter', some critics believing that it refers to the person who principally inspired the sonnets, and thus seeking to identify Mr W.H. with the young man in the sequence. It is possible that 'begetter' means nothing more than the person who obtained the manuscript for the publisher, but, nevertheless, a great deal of energy has been devoted to discovering the identity of the mysterious Mr W.H. Among the main contenders for this role are William Harvey, William Hatcliffe, William Herbert, William Hall, and Henry Wriothesley (reversing the initials), Earl of Southampton. The claims of the first four candidates are strengthened by the frequent puns on 'Will' in the later sonnets. However, Southampton's known patronage of Shakespeare has made him a favourite candidate, alongside William Herbert, one of the noblemen to whom the first collected edition of Shakespeare's plays was dedicated in 1623. The problem is unlikely to be solved.†

---

* In *The Sonnets*, edited by William Burto, The Signet Classic Shakespeare, New American Library, London, 1964, p.xx.
† See K. Muir, *Shakespeare's Sonnets*, Allen & Unwin, London, 1979, pp.152–5.

Although we know the date of publication of the first edition of the sonnets, there is little evidence about the date of their composition. The sonnets contain numerous instances of links with other works by Shakespeare (notably with the comedy *Love's Labour's Lost*), but there is no reason to assume that this means that Shakespeare wrote these sonnets at the same time as this play: he may have anticipated the play in the sonnets, or echoed the play long after its composition.

The vogue of the sonnet sequence was short-lived, and this might argue for a date of composition early in the 1590s. This is supported by the fact that Shakespeare's early comedies, dating from this period, include satire of the fashion of writing sonnets. Links between Shakespeare's sonnets and his plays are dealt with later in this section.

Ordering

The 1609 edition of the sonnets is flawed: it fails to reach a satisfactory conclusion, and certain individual sonnets are in need of revision. Because of this critics have been tempted to challenge the order of the sequence in this edition. This temptation is difficult to resist because the sonnets (unlike, for example, a play) have no single line of narrative and it is thus open to readers to see in the sonnets whatever line of narrative they will, and to suggest re-ordering the sonnets to fit their hypothesis. Nevertheless, however many different orderings are suggested, most critics prefer to trust in the sequence published in 1609, and the integrity of the ordering is re-affirmed as each year passes and critics perceive links between sonnets which had not been evident before. Attempts to suggest alternative orderings often destroy more links than they forge: see, for example, the note to sonnet 40 in Part 2.

Nineteenth-century critics were disturbed by some of the sonnets because they did not seem to be morally uplifting (often, indeed, they seem to be quite the reverse), and thus they suggested that these poems were either inferior or not by Shakespeare at all. Many of their qualms arose from the fear of these critics that the poems might celebrate homosexual love: it is possible, however, to react less violently if one is prepared to accept that the poems are not necessarily autobiographical, and that Shakespeare's decision to treat the subject of love between men might arise from his desire to explore and expand the conventions of the sonnet as fully as possible.

Conventions

The notes and glossaries in Part 2 of these Notes are by no means complete. No set of notes could ever hope thoroughly to gloss every nuance of such complex poetry as that in Shakespeare's sonnets. Each sonnet must be carefully read and examined for such recurrent complexities as the ambiguous use of 'dear', 'fair', and 'love'. 'Dear is consistently used both in the sense of 'beloved' and as 'expensive'; this is true, for example, in sonnet 87:

> Farewell, thou art too dear for my possessing
> And like enough thou know'st thy estimate.

The sonnet proceeds to play upon both senses of 'dear' throughout its fourteen lines. In a similar way, sonnet 127 exploits the ambiguity of 'fair': meaning 'light-haired', 'beautiful', and 'just'. The most frequent play, however, is upon the word 'love', which can refer either to the emotion or to the beloved person: this ambiguity gives extra complexity to such phrases as: 'mine own love's strength' (sonnet 23) (either the strength of my feelings, or the strength of my beloved); 'my love's picture' (sonnet 47) (either a portrait of my beloved, or a copy of my feelings); 'weep afresh love's long since cancelled woe' (sonnet 30) (either weep again for the pain of love, or weep for a new beloved). Examples such as these should encourage readers to be alert to the possibility of ambiguity in every sonnet. Many of the problems of ambiguity can be resolved by reading the sonnets in the context of the sequence as a whole: even such a difficult sonnet as sonnet 94 makes more sense in the light of those sonnets which come before and after it, a fact to which too few critics have paid attention. Some sonnets, indeed, can only make sense in the light of the preceding sonnet: those such as 16 and 92 which begin with 'But' quite clearly flow on from the preceding sonnet, continuing the same argument while developing the central idea in a new direction.

Shakespeare's sonnets are striking in that they often speak directly to the object of love, the young man or the Dark Lady. The sonnets of his predecessors tended to use the third person form of address. Sidney, however, includes some examples of direct address in *Astrophil and Stella*, for example, in sonnet 14: 'Alas, have I not pain enough, my friend'. Thus Shakespeare's technique here is one instance of his developing a trait which was implicit in the work of an earlier sonneteer. This development of convention is fundamental to Shakespeare's sonnets.

Conceit

One basic feature of the sonnet is its reliance upon paradox. The situations described in sonnets are often paradoxical and it is the paradox to which the reader often responds. For example, this sonnet by Sidney expresses a conflict of emotions which must have been felt by generations of lovers the world over:

When I was forst from *Stella* ever deere,
Stella, food of my thoughts, hart of my hart,
Stella whose eyes make all my tempests cleere,
By iron lawes of duty to depart:
Alas I found, that she with me did smart,
I saw that teares did in her eyes appeare;
I saw that sighes her sweetest lips did part,
And her sad words my sadded sence did heare.
For me, I wept to see pearles scattered so,
I sighd her sighes, and wailed for her wo,
Yet swam in joy, such love in her was seene
Thus while th'effect most bitter was to me,
And nothing then the cause more sweet could be,
I had bene vext, if vext I had not beene.*

The conflict between sadness at the lady's suffering and joy that she suffers for the poet, is a classic paradox of the sonnet tradition. The placing of such opposites as 'bitter' and 'sweet' side by side, and the suggestion that both can be true at the same time, is one example of a common feature of the sonnet known as the conceit.

Shakespeare uses the word 'conceit' in one of its senses in sonnet 15 when he writes:

the conceit of this inconstant stay
Sets you most rich in youth before my sight

As a literary term, 'conceit' means more than 'thought' although it is very much concerned with the intellectual process. A conceit is an argument, a comparison, or a description which surprises the reader and challenges him by its intellectual contrast. Shakespeare makes frequent use of minor conceits similar to that in the Sidney sonnet above. In sonnet 47, for example, Shakespeare argues that his absent love is still with him, which leads to the paradox; 'Thyself away are present still with me'. Sonnet 75, similarly, expresses a conflict of emotions which is reflected in a paradox:

Thus do I pine and surfeit day by day
Or gluttoning on all, or all away

A more extended conceit occurs in sonnet 22, in which the poet is attempting to prove that he and the young man are one and the same person and that he will therefore take special care of himself because, in doing so, he is caring for the young man. The notion of proving is a vital ingredient of the conceit, which is essentially an attempt to prove something which is extremely unlikely or positively untrue (such as that

* *The Poems of Sir Philip Sidney*, pp.222–3.

the poet is no older than the young man): the pleasure derived from the conceit is in an admiration of the ingenuity with which the poet makes his case.

One sub-division of the conceit is the blazon, which Shakespeare refers to in sonnet 106, and which he parodies in sonnet 130, in which, according to convention, the physical attributes of the lady are compared to the parts of some other object. Sonnet 18 is an example of the way in which Shakespeare develops the blazon, not merely comparing his beloved to a summer's day, but pointing out the differences between the two which make his love superior. Occasionally the lover will wish himself an object which is in close proximity with his beloved, as Romeo envies Juliet's glove:

> See! how she leans her cheek upon her hand:
> O! that I were a glove upon that hand,
> That I might touch that cheek. (II, ii, 23−5)*

Shakespeare develops this kind of conceit in sonnet 128, although, again, he moves beyond the convention to make his envy of the musical instrument played by his mistress an oblique criticism of her promiscuity.

A frequent conceit in this sequence is that based upon hypothesis, in which the poet imagines what might happen in some future time. Sonnets employing this kind of conceit begin either with 'If', or, more usually, 'When'.

Possibly the main sub-group of the conceit is that concerned with the passage of time, in which the poet uses the swift passage of time as an argument for his lady to surrender to his seduction. This tradition is known as *carpe diem* (seize the day) and is a conceit which was originated by the Roman poet Horace (65−8 BC) and is widely found in English literature. Shakespeare draws upon this tradition in, for example, *Venus and Adonis* and *Twelfth Night*. In his sonnets, Shakespeare makes such frequent reference to time that the topic needs to be discussed separately later in this section. This prominent feature of the sequence is a development of the conceit, and a very sophisticated development at that.

Imagery

Imagery is probably the feature of language which we most associate with poetry and its use in the sonnet is worth our close attention. In discussing imagery it is useful to distinguish between the tenor (the substance of the message), and the vehicle (the comparison used to

---

* Quoted in J.A. Cuddon, *A Dictionary of Literary Terms*, André Deutsch, London, 1979, p.145.

convey that message). Thus, in sonnet 8, Shakespeare attempts to convince the young man that he should wed by pointing to the example of harmony in music:

> Mark how one string, sweet husband to another,
> Strikes each in each by mutual ordering:
> Resembling sire, and child, and happy mother,
> Who all in one, one pleasing note do sing

The tenor of these lines is that marriage leads not to division but to mutual agreement and satisfaction. The vehicle is the image of musical harmony.

In a sequence as lengthy as that of Shakespeare's sonnets there is the opportunity for the poet to develop the relationship between tenor and vehicle in a varied and interesting way. Thus, for example, not only do we find the same tenor being expressed through different vehicles (the many analogies used, for example, to convince the young man that he should marry), but also the same vehicle being used to express different tenors. For example, images of eyes and of blood recur throughout the sonnets but are not consistently carrying the same tenor. Eyes can be representative of the resemblance between child and parent (sonnet 2), of the opinion of others (sonnet 29), or of the sun (sonnet 7). Similarly, images of blood can be used to represent the colour of a beautiful cheek (82), the life-force that passes from one generation to another (11), or the horror of death and destruction (129). Other recurrent images which would repay detailed study are those of day and night, seasons, and legal and accounting images.

In addition to noticing the kind of image being used, we need also to be sensitive to the way in which imagery is being employed. Some sonnets, for example, are sparing in their use of imagery and thus the first lines in which an image does occur are given greater prominence: sonnet 29 is a good example of this technique. Some sonnets will be quite self-contained in their imagery, being based upon a single image which is not used in any of the surrounding sonnets: sonnets 7 and 143 exemplify this technique (and each begins with 'Lo', an indication that a single simile is to dominate the poem). In contrast, other sonnets employ a variety of images drawn from other sonnets in the immediate context: sonnet 6 is a good example of this principle, which is common throughout the sequence. Finally, Shakespeare occasionally startles the reader by blurring the distinction between tenor and vehicle so that the reader is persuaded that he is reading the tenor when in fact he is being presented only with a vehicle: thus sonnet 33 appears in its octave to be a record of the poet's experience of changeable weather, and yet the sestet makes it clear that the opening has merely been a vehicle to describe this young man's fickleness.

People and situations

In the peopling of his sonnet sequence Shakespeare is at his most innovative. On the basis of a sequence like *Astrophil and Stella* one might look for the poet to describe himself fully, to write of a beautiful, unattainable lady of superior social rank, to fear a rival lover, and, perhaps, to speak occasionally to a friend (to reject his rational advice). In Shakespeare's sequences the bulk of the sonnets (including, arguably, the most effective) are addressed to a young man, the lady is promiscuous and derided, and the rival is a rival poet. These people are, in all probability, creatures of the poet's imagination just as much as 'the poet' is almost certainly not to be identified with Shakespeare himself. As Stephen Booth shrewdly observes: 'William Shakespeare was almost certainly homosexual, bisexual, or heterosexual. The sonnets provide no evidence on the matter.'*

The young man is a direct descendant of the ladies in earlier sonnet sequences. He is beautiful, as they are; he is the poet's social superior as they are; the poet's love for the young man is hopeless, as is the love of other's poets for their ladies. However, the sequence cannot be read intelligently merely by imagining that the young man is a girl, or by following the practice of Benson's 1640 edition and changing 'he' to 'she'. Although the young man may be as cruel as any lady (he has power of life and death over the poet in sonnet 40), it is a vital part of the structure of the sequence that he is a man. The poems to the young man are not poems of courtship or homosexual seduction: the poet does not attempt to persuade the young man to surrender to him. He invites the young man to surrender to marriage and to bear children. Thus Shakespeare is being innovative not only in failing to write a seduction sequence (the ultimate goal of his love is that the young man should marry another), but also in writing a sequence in which marriage and children play so prominent a part. The traditional sonneteers never looked beyond courtship: marriage seemed impossible (especially as the lady was already married), and anything after marriage was unthinkable.

The role of the poet in relation to the young man is thought out with equal care. He is a man talking to another man, and can therefore deal with topics (such as having children) which would be too indelicate for a conventional sequence addressed to a lady. He is also dependent upon his beloved in more than the conventional way. The traditional sonneteer may claim that his lady is all life holds for him, but the poet of Shakespeare's sequence is materially and financially dependent upon the young man, for he is his patron as well as lord of his heart.

* *Shakespeare's Sonnets*, edited by Stephen Booth, Yale University Press, New Haven and London, 1977, p.548.

The poet represents himself as older than the young man (Shakespeare himself was probably under thirty when he wrote the sonnets), and this becomes a useful guise which enables the sonnets on death and morality to gain in poignancy and relevance whilst also adding to the complexity of the relationship between poet and young man. Older people might be expected to give advice to their more youthful friends, but this is set against the poet's lowly social status: in a chronological sense, then, the poet is the young man's senior, but socially he is his dependant. Thus the minor paradoxes occurring in individual sonnets are reflected in this larger paradox of relationships which dominates the whole sequence.

The relationship between the poet and the Dark Lady is equally unconventional, if rather less complex. He speaks to her, and of her, in a most uncourtly and unromantic manner. Not only is she attainable by him but by almost everybody, and his love for her, far from elevating him spiritually, drives him to the despair of sonnet 129.

Jan Kott identifies a further character latent in Shakespeare's sequence: 'The fourth character of the drama is time. Time which destroys and devours everything.'* Shakespeare's inclusion of this fourth character is a development of the *carpe diem* conceit and the presentation of time in the sonnets is ambivalent. On the one hand, time destroys, but, on the other, it is through time that everything, including love itself, grows and develops. A poem in the *carpe diem* tradition urges nothing more than living for the moment, making the most of youth and beauty while it lasts. Shakespeare, however, is as much concerned with the future as with the present: he is not merely urging the young man to enjoy himself now, but to consider his future and the future of his family. He is concerned with defeating time, not just with using time's destruction as an argument for seduction. This feature above all makes Shakespeare's sequence distinctive and makes the poet its central figure. The poet is himself central to any sonnet sequence. We learn far more of Astrophil than of Stella in Sidney's sequence, and more of the poet than of the young man or the Dark Lady in Shakespeare's. Tradition would lead us to expect little detailed description, but Shakespeare develops even this feature by explaining exactly why he will not describe either of the objects of his love: his mistress is all too obviously not beautiful, and the young man's beauty makes him dumb. The only voice we hear is that of the poet: even in sonnet 32, for example, where the young man appears to speak, the situation is hypothetical, and the lines are therefore imagined by the poet; and even that minor character, the rival poet, is, in being a poet, an extension of the poet's own self.

* Jan Kott, *Shakespeare our Contemporary*, Methuen, London, 1965, p.191.

The sonnet form

By the late sixteenth century the sonnet form was highly developed and a poet could select from a wide range of possible rhyme-schemes. Shakespeare's sonnets, however, are remarkably uniform in that scarcely any of them deviate from the scheme

a b a b c d c d e f e f g g

Shakespeare's development of the formal features of the sonnet did not lie in his experimentation with rhyme. He was innovative in his use of extensive linkage between sonnets, both in the syntactic linkage between, for example, sonnets 15 and 16, and also in the prevalent use of linked imagery. His rhymes are not, however, entirely without interest: for example, sonnet 3 reinforces its message that the young man can cheat death through marriage by emphasising the contrast in the rhymes 'womb' and 'tomb'. Sonnet 55 is concerned with various kinds of memorials and their impermanence. Although it does not use the word 'tomb', it prepares our expectations for the word by the rhymes 'room' and 'doom'. Sonnet 86 completes the process by juxtaposing 'tomb' and 'womb' in the same line and forcing our attention back to sonnet 3.

A further feature of Shakespeare's technique is the way he exploits the reader's expectations.* Frequently he writes a line which appears to make complete sense on its own, only for the reader to discover that the line continues and means something quite different. Sonnet 15, for example, begins 'When I consider everything that grows' and it appears that this is a complete statement: the poet is thinking about all growing things. However, the sense does not stop at the end of the line for, reading on, we discover that the sentence continues

> When I consider everything that grows
> Holds in perfection but a little moment

The reader can now see that the sense is 'When I consider that everything which grows holds its perfection only briefly.' Sonnets 84 and 133 have similar opening lines which appear end-stopped, but do, in fact, run on.

Poems and plays

It is hardly surprising that there are connections between Shakespeare's poems and his plays. Most writers have preoccupations which recur again and again in their work, and there are abundant links in themes within Shakespeare's plays. Moreover, there are close stylistic

---

* See Stephen Booth, *An Essay on Shakespeare's Sonnets*, Yale University Press, New Haven and London, 1969, p.181.

links: the iambic pentameter, the ten-syllable line common in English poetry, can take one of three possible forms, two of which (blank verse and the heroic couplet) are the basis of Shakespeare's verse in his plays; the other form is the sonnet itself.

Thus we find that a sonnet can slip into the texture of a scene in a play without our noticing its presence: Kenneth Muir* suggests that such a passage as this from *Love's Labour's Lost*, embedded in a speech by Berowne, may in itself be a sonnet:

> Study me how to please the eye indeed,
> By fixing it upon a fairer eye;
> Who dazzling so, that eye shall be his heed,
> And give him light that it was blinded by.
> Study is like the heaven's glorious sun,
> That will not be deep-search'd with saucy looks;
> Small have continual plodders ever won,
> Save base authority from others' books.
> These earthly godfathers of heaven's lights
> That give a name to every fixed star
> Have no more profit of their shining nights
> Than those that walk and wot not what they are.
> Too much to know is to know nought but fame;
> And every godfather can give a name.   (I, i, 80–93)

More obviously, *Romeo and Juliet*, a play which opens with a sonnet from the Chorus, marks the meeting of the lovers by having them speak a sonnet together which reaches a climax in their first kiss (*Romeo and Juliet*, Act I, Scene 5, lines 96—109).

Shakespeare's early comedies contain numerous satiric references to the fashionable lovelorn young man, pining for his unattainable mistress, some of which refer explicitly to the writing of sonnets as part of the lover's typical behaviour. Thus Berowne announces that he is not a lover in these terms:

> When shall you see me write a thing in rhyme?
> Or groan for Joan? Or spend a minute's time
> In pruning me?   (IV, iii, 177–9)

Berowne, in fact, has already composed one of the three overt sonnets written by the young man in the play, and these plays contain numerous echoes of the language of the sonnets (or perhaps the sonnets echo the plays), including most notably the fact that Berowne's love is herself a Dark Lady, whose beauty must be defended against the conventions of the time and proved:

* K. Muir, *Shakespeare's Sonnets*, Allen & Unwin, London, 1979, p.132.

O, if in black my lady's brows be deckt,
It mourns that painting and usurping hair
Should ravish doters with a false aspect;
And therefore is she born to make black fair.
Her favour turns the fashion of the days;
For native blood is counted painting now;
And therefore red that would avoid dispraise
Paints itself black, to imitate her brow.   (IV, iii, 254–61)

In his plays as well as in his non-dramatic poetry Shakespeare refuses to write conventionally of love, and, in the comedies, scarcely ever takes it seriously. We find in the plays a similar development of the conventions as we find in the sonnets, and a similar exploitation of the audience's expectations. In *Love's Labour's Lost* the audience is led to expect that, at the end of the play, the four young men will wed the four young ladies: this is the manner in which comedies of love might be expected to end. However, not only does Shakespeare not allow the play to reach this conclusion, but his principal character, Berowne, makes it clear that he knows he is going against dramatic convention:

Our wooing doth not end like an old play:
Jack hath not Jill. These ladies' courtesy
Might well have made our sport a comedy.   (V, ii, 862–4)

In other plays Shakespeare complicates the wooing and the romance by having one or more of his characters in disguise, this often involving a girl being dressed as a man. Thus Rosalind in *As You Like It* disguises herself as Ganymede and finds to her cost that Phebe falls in love with her. Again the prospect of a straightforward story of a boy wooing a girl is developed by Shakespeare into something altogether different. In *The Taming of the Shrew* there appears to be some trace of a simple story of romantic love in the wooing of Bianca, the apparently docile sister of the shrewish Katherina. It appears that Bianca's story is being used as a marked contrast to the unromantic wooing of Katherina by Petruchio, who unashamedly confesses that he wants her for her money. Ultimately, however, it is clear that Bianca is as shrewish as her sister and that her husband may not have obtained such a prize after all. Thus, throughout his comedies we see Shakespeare innovating, and challenging the expectations of his audience.

One of Shakespeare's most frequent preoccupations is with the presentation of variations of conventional love. Even in his earliest published poem, *Venus and Adonis*, he refuses to stick slavishly to his classical sources and makes his Venus a large and vigorous goddess who rapaciously pursues a vain and self-regarding Adonis. Part of the humour in this poem arises from the fact that the expected sexual roles are reversed. However, even the reversal does not entirely explain the effect of the poem, for Adonis is not merely coy (as the beloved lady in a conventional poem ought to be), but actually quite unattractive in his personality. The poem's interest does not lie merely in its comedy, however, for it has touches of seriousness unusual in a mythological narrative: Venus's arguments are carefully refuted by Adonis, who discriminates shrewdly between love and lust:

> Love comforteth like sunshine after rain,
> But Lust's effect is tempest after sun;
> Love's gentle spring doth always fresh remain:
> Lust's winter comes ere summer half be done.

(lines 799–802)

Such a distinction is rare in a poem of this kind.

The presentation of sexuality

In *Venus and Adonis* Shakespeare is using the reversal of the expected sexual roles in order to investigate human sexuality. The poem shocks us into re-evaluating our attitude to female sexuality and forces us to ask whether a woman might take the initiative in courtship as Venus does, and, if she did, whether we would think her ridiculous.

Shakespeare's plays frequently concern themselves with investigations of sexuality, investigations arising partly from the stage conventions of the time. In the Elizabethan and Jacobean theatres women did not appear on the stage, female roles being played by young boys. Shakespeare was perceptive enough to appreciate that the spectacle of a stage lover attempting to seduce a 'lady' who was in reality a boy might have very real potential, both in terms of comic confusion and for a serious enquiry into sexuality. His exploiting of comic potential can be illustrated in the induction to *The Taming of the Shrew*, where the drunkard Christopher Sly is dressed up as a Lord and provided with a 'wife' who is in fact a young page boy. The audience of Shakespeare's day would have appreciated the fact that all of the 'women' in the play were in fact as false as Sly's 'wife'.

In a later comedy, *Twelfth Night*, the convention is exploited for a more serious purpose. Viola, the heroine, is forced to disguise herself as a boy and enter the service of the Duke Orsino. Thus we have, in terms of the Elizabethan stage, a boy acting the part of a girl pretending to be a boy. This boy-girl, Viola, becomes the focus of the attention of the other major characters. Ultimately she is married to Orsino, but it is made quite clear that Orsino has been very attracted to her whilst she was pretending to be a boy, and that she has also won the heart of the Lady Olivia whilst in disguise. In one of the most poignant scenes in the play Olivia declares her love to the unfortunate Viola who can only protest that the love is hopeless. Here Shakespeare is taking the conventional situation of a love which can never be attained, and extending it into one in which consummation is impossible for quite different reasons.* At the end of *Twelfth Night*, as Orsino prepares to marry Viola, and Olivia goes off with Sebastian, Viola's brother, the characters ought to feel less than certain about their sexual identity: Orsino has been very attached to what he thought was boy, and Olivia has declared her love for someone who now appears as a woman.

Twelfth Night is by no means the only Shakespearean comedy to pursue unconventional views of sexuality: the friendship between Antonio and Bassanio in *The Merchant of Venice* matters every bit as much as Bassanio's courtship of Portia. Plays such as these prepare us for the sonnets by introducing a writer not limited merely to the conventional love-themes. In Shakespeare men may love men, women may love women, and some characters may even love themselves. Malvolio, the steward in *Twelfth Night*, is described as 'sick of self-love' but he is by no means the only character to suffer from this disease. Many of the protagonists in Shakespeare's plays are searching for part of their identity, like Antipholus of Syracuse in *A Comedy of Errors*:

> I, to find a mother and a brother.
> In quest of them, unhappy, lose myself.   (I, ii, 39–40)

Shakespeare's sonnets show a similar concern with identity as the poet considers how much the young man resembles himself, how much he resembles his mother, and how much both poet and young man are reflected in the Dark Lady. It is possible to read the whole sequence as a debate between the pure emotion of disinterested friendship and the degradation of lust (a similar tension between friendship and sexuality is portrayed in *The Two Gentlemen of Verona*). Shakespeare's development of the sonnet sequence in addressing so many of the sonnets to the young man allows him to discuss topics such as marriage and children which would have been considered indelicate in a sequence conventionally addressed to a lady.

Poems about poems

Much of the best poetry of the Elizabethan period confronts the difficult question of the relationship between art and reality, and the usefulness of poetry itself. Sonneteers were no exception to this trend. Poets increasingly used sonnet sequences to express their views about the function of poetry; they explored in sonnets the possibility that art

* A further feature of the relationships in *Twelfth Night* which adds to their complexity and bears comparison with the sonnets is that Viola, in posing as Cesario, makes herself the social inferior of Olivia and Orsino.

could transcend mortality by making statements which would last for all time. Shakespeare, like Sidney before him, is anxious to claim that his sonnets are the product of original invention, not dependent upon the examples of earlier sonneteers, and that they will stand as a lasting memorial to his beloved even when all other memorials have faded. Shakespeare, however, does not consistently argue that his sonnets will survive: even in the group of sonnets 12 to 18 we can see a variation in the content of his argument. But it is necessary to be aware of the extent to which Shakespeare is continually reminding his readers of the fact that they are reading synthetic products, works of art, which, however highly wrought, are fictions and quite separate from reality. Take, for instance, a sonnet such as 21, which disclaims all artifice:

> O let me true in love but truly write,
> And then believe me, my love is as fair
> As any mother's child, though not so bright
> As those gold candles fixed in heaven's air.
> Let them say more that like of hearsay well;
> I will not praise that purpose not to sell.

This sonnet itself belongs to a traditional mode of sonnets feigning spontaneity (like, for example, Sidney's sonnet 15, quoted in Part 1 of these Notes), and serves to heighten our appreciation of the extent to which the poet is doing the reverse of what he claims. Shakespeare, skilful artist that he is, can afford to remind his readers that his poems are artificial, just as in his plays he reminds his audience that they are watching drama not reality. This is yet a further reason why we should reject any interpretation of his sonnets that suggests that they are auto-biographical. An Iris Murdoch novel* includes the following exchange between a critic and a student:

> 'When is Shakespeare at his most cryptic?'
> 'How do you mean?'
> 'What is the most mysterious and endlessly debated part of his oeuvre?'
> 'The sonnets?'
> 'Correct.'

The fact that the critic goes on to suggest that the difficulty of the sonnets derives from the fact that Shakespeare is writing about himself is an indication of just how bad a critic he is.

---

* Iris Murdoch, *The Black Prince*, Chatto & Windus, London, 1973, pp.162–3.

Part 4

Hints for study

IN PREPARING SHAKESPEARE'S SONNETS for examination purposes it is necessary to be able to focus on a range of individual sonnets large enough to be representative and yet small enough to hold in your mind. It would be impossible to have a close acquaintance with all 154 sonnets: some are far more well-known than others and deservedly so. Part 3 of these Notes is intended to provide a background for and an introduction to the sequence as a whole; this section will attempt to demonstrate how close attention to about a dozen carefully selected sonnets should arm you sufficiently to allow you to write confidently on any questions set.

The kinds of questions relevant to a study of the sonnets will be concerned either with the ideas contained in the poems, or with the manner of presentation of those ideas. The principal themes of Shakespeare's sonnets are the difference between the poet's feelings for the young man and those for the Dark Lady; Time and the extent to which anything can be permanent; poetry itself; and the originality of the poet's work. Questions on presentation will also include some consideration of at least the last two of these categories: Shakespeare is often deliberately emphasising the restrictions of the sonnet form, underlining the conventions which he has inherited from earlier poets by inverting those conventions. Other issues of presentation would include the kinds of imagery employed in the sonnets, and the viewpoint from which the sonnet is written. All of these issues of theme and presentation are exemplified below with respect to particular sonnets.

One extremely useful technique for gaining a close acquaintance with the sonnets is to practise reading them aloud, especially if that reading can be done by more than one person. Many of Shakespeare's sonnets display the same complexity of structure that was noted in Sidney's sonnet 15 from *Astrophil and Stella* in Part 1 of these Notes, and that complexity can be illuminated by experimenting with different ways of reading the sonnets aloud. For example, it would be possible to emphasise the complex structure of sonnet 29 by dividing between two voices and attempting two quite separate readings: one in which each voice reads four lines each in turn, plus the final couplet; and a second reading in which one voice reads the octave and the other the sestet. The first of these readings is truer to the rhyme-scheme of the poem, but makes a break between lines 4 and 5 which the sense of the poem does not allow. The second reading shows the true pattern of the theme, emphasising the turn in the argument at the beginning of line 9. Another useful experiment is to have two voices reading alternate lines: by this means it is possible to discover the extent to which separate lines make sense on their own, and the proportion of lines which need to be continued in order to make sense. The opening line of sonnet 29, for example, cannot stand on its own and make sense: it is an incomplete statement. The opening line of sonnet 130, on the other hand, is a full clause and makes complete sense.

The sonnets that repay particularly careful attention and, taken together, provide a fair representation of the sequence as a whole are sonnets 15, 16, 18, 20, 29, 55, 73, 116, 129, 130 and 144.

Sonnet 15 is a good example of one of the major thematic concerns of the sequence: the negative effects of time. This theme is by no means simple and other sonnets in the group under consideration will develop and extend the theme. In this sonnet the emphasis of the octave is upon the inevitability of time's destruction: every living thing on earth is affected by it. We might expect that there would be a shift in the argument at the beginning of line 9 (as we have grown used to in the sonnets). Some aspects of the patterning of the sonnet encourages us in this view: lines 1 and 5 begin with 'When', whereas line 9 begins with 'Then' and this might lead us to expect the establishing of one set of principles, followed by their reversal. This reversal, however, does not take place: the sestet does not describe a source of consolation (for example, that the beauty of the beloved might defeat time), but instead it reinforces the pessimism of the octave. When the poet thinks of the destruction caused by time he is reminded that the beauty of love is under attack from time. The sonnet hardly contains a turn in the argument at all: there is the slight implication of a turn in the final line, as the poet suggests that the only means of defeating time is through his poetry. However, this sonnet does not (as others do) emphasise very forcibly the power of poetry to achieve immortality: this section of the sequence questions the permanence of poetry. Indeed the true turn in the argument occurs at the beginning of the sonnet which follows (*sonnet 16*), where the poet argues that a better way of defeating Time would be for the young man to marry and to have a child: the natural cycle of ageing and death can only be defeated by the natural cycle of birth and growth. This sonnet suggests that the creative act of producing children is superior to the creative activity of producing art. Thus these two sonnets touch on the theme of time, poetry, and the relationship between art and nature, as well as demonstrating aspects of Shakespeare's sonnet technique.

Sonnet 18 is an illustration of Shakespeare's exploiting of sonnet convention. Again the sonnet is concerned with time's destruction, asserting that everything must decay and that only poetry can last. In this sonnet, however, the power of poetry to last forever is not questioned, although some of the conventions of sonnets are under attack from Shakespeare. The sonnet opens with the poet considering whether or not to employ a conventional comparison, the comparison between the young man and a summer's day. The poet finds this comparison inadequate because a summer's day is itself far from perfect: summer fades inevitably into winter but the beauty of the young man can be preserved through the poet's description.

Sonnet 20 is a different kind of poem in which the tone is much more lighthearted than in the previous three which we have considered. This sonnet considers the resemblance between the young man and a conventional mistress, and has some harsh things to say about women in the comparison it makes. Again Shakespeare is demonstrating his mastery of the sonnet technique by introducing this variation of tone. Conventionally we might expect sonnets to be reverential in their attitude to women, but here the bawdiness (especially in the final couplet) undercuts any sense that women are superior to men.

Sonnet 29 introduces the issue of viewpoint and stance: most sonnets claim to be about the beloved, or about the emotion of love; this sonnet, however, is more preoccupied with the poet himself than most. The movement and dynamism in this sonnet comes from the contrast between the initial self-absorption of the poet (his preoccupation with his own bad fortune) and the final joy that the thought of the young man brings to him. This change is marked by a change in imagery: the octave is almost devoid of any image while the poet thinks only of himself. When, however, he remembers his love for the young man, the sestet can include a beautiful comparison between his rising emotions and a soaring lark. This sonnet can be included in our selected group because it deals with the poet's uncertain place in society and introduces the theme of patronage.

Sonnet 55 is another sonnet concerned with the power of poetry to defeat time, here with no apparent reservations about the permanence of a poem. The octave is concerned with other kinds of memorials (statues, monuments, and tombs) and finds that they can be destroyed, whereas poetry cannot. There is a certain irony in the description of the possible destruction of such tangible and solid objects as statues in contrast to the claim that such a fragile thing as a poem might survive. The basis of the claim is that the poet's feelings for the young man will last forever because they will be re-lived by future generations of lovers.

Sonnet 73 is like sonnet 29 in that it concentrates upon the poet himself. The sonnet is about old age (and therefore can hardly be about

Shakespeare himself) and may appear at first glance to be somewhat repetitive in structure. It seems to have three quatrains and couplet, each quatrain containing a different image of age. A closer reading, however, reveals that each quatrain is varied in the extent to which the meaning or tenor of the image is revealed. The first quatrain contains no simple statement of the meaning: it describes an autumnal scene, and refers back to what that scene had once been. The second quatrain is concerned with time rather than place and does include, in its final line, an explanation of the meaning of the image: 'Death's second self, that seals up all in rest.' The third quatrain is concerned with the abstract quality, the fire of life itself, and includes a two-line reference to death. Thus, as the poem progresses, its mood becomes increasingly sombre as the references to death become more explicit.

Sonnet 116 is the last sonnet in our select group to be concerned primarily with the relationship with the young man. It is a poem of definition, developing a comprehensive statement about the nature of love. Questions of technique are again relevant here: the first quatrain is concerned with defining what love is not, the second with defining the positive qualities of love, and the third with combining positive and negative definitions. This sonnet is less tied to particular circumstances than the others considered so far: there is no direct reference to the young man or to the poet himself. Indeed the final couplet of the sonnet claims that its definitions are universally true. The sonnet is principally concerned with the permanent and unchanging nature of love and may therefore be linked with other sonnets on the theme of time. In this case it is not poetry or children that can defeat time but love itself, which lasts forever.

Sonnet 129 is one of the most despairing of the whole sequence. It is concerned not with love but with lust, the simple animal passion devoid of any tenderness or caring emotion. Part of the effect of the sonnet comes from the absence of a conventional turning point at the beginning of line 9: it forms an interesting comparison with sonnet 116 in that it consists of a series of definitions. However, this sonnet is much more direct and abrupt in its definitions, consisting of broken, disjointed lines which describe every aspect of love in negative terms. It is an explicit reversal of the accepted sonnet argument that love leads men to heaven, here emphasising the degradation that comes from lust.

Sonnet 130 is also deliberately anti-conventional, since it takes the typical blazon of the lady's beauty and denies that it applies to the Dark Lady. However, although the poet does not adopt the traditional tone of reverence towards the lady (indeed the tone is quite light-hearted), the impression given by the final couplet is of a sincere tribute to his mistress which is superior to the conventional blazons of earlier sonneteers.

Sonnet 144 explicitly compares the poet's two loves: for the young man and for the dark lady. It finds that the love for the young man is superior, in that its associations are angelic and pure. The situation (of the young man's infidelity) is first mentioned in sonnets 40, 41 and 42, and developed (from a new perspective) in 133 and 134. In this sonnet the difference between the young man and the Dark Lady is most clearly emphasised through the contrasting images of angel and devil.

A close acquaintance with the sonnets discussed above ought to provide a sufficient basis to answer any essay question set on the sequence. The list below summarises the salient features of these sonnets:

Sonnet
15/16 War with Time: challenging of sonnet convention: poetry impermanent
18 Challenging of sonnet convention: poetry permanent
20 Challenging of sonnet convention: comparison of men and women
29 Poet's self
55 War with Time: investigation of love: poetry permanent
73 Poet's self: death
116 War with Time: investigation of love
129 Challenging of sonnet convention: love and lust
130 Challenging of sonnet convention
144 Comparison of men and women

Sample essay questions

(1) With reference to particular sonnets, illustrate the ways in which Shakespeare develops the theme of the war against time.
(2) To what extent do Shakespeare's sonnets rely upon conventions used by earlier sonneteers?
(3) Compare and contrast the presentation of the young man and the Dark Lady.
(4) What do Shakespeare's sonnets tell us about the nature of poetry itself?
(5) 'Although the sonnets are not autobiographical, the person of the Poet makes a significant contribution to their success.' Discuss the way in which the Poet is presented.
(6) Consider the means by which Shakespeare achieves a range and variety of effects within the limits of the sonnet form.
(7) In what ways are Shakespeare's sonnets dependent upon, or enhanced by, the context of being set in a sequence?

(8) C.S. Lewis wrote that a good sonnet was 'like a good prayer . . . the test is whether the congregation can "join" and make it their own'. Do Shakespeare's sonnets conform to this definition?

Specimen answer

(6) Consider the means by which Shakespeare achieves a range and variety of effects within the limits of the sonnet form.

When Shakespeare wrote his sonnet sequence the fashion for sonnets was drawing to a close: during the previous ten years sonneteers had flourished and the sonnet had become the accepted form in which a poet could play the part of a lover addressing his lady. So popular was this practice that Shakespeare could satirise it in a number of his early comedies.

In choosing to write this particular form of poem, the poet has chosen to accept a number of constraints both in theme and in style, and these conventions, together with the sheer bulk of sonnets produced in the Elizabethan period, might make it seem virtually impossible for a poet to achieve any measure of originality within the form. However, Shakespeare succeeded in writing an original sonnet sequence, partly through his exploiting conventions of style and partly through the ingenuity he displays in devising new situations for the sonnet sequence.

Many earlier sequences had claimed to be spontaneous, original, and unconventional, although none of them can be taken to be autobiographical. However sincere the poet may claim to be, he is, in writing sonnets, displaying his skill within the poem: his love is not real; it is merely part of the convention. Shakespeare's sonnets cannot be taken as autobiographical, and in the sequence he is developing the convention by peopling his sonnets in an original manner. The traditional sonnet had as its central theme the concept of an ideal courtship: the poet expressing his love for an idealised, unattainable lady. In Shakespeare's sequence the object of devotion is a young man, the friend and patron of the poet, and the lady is relegated to play a subordinate role in the sequence. This change in the characters of the sequence makes Shakespeare's sonnets appear much more frank and personal. Earlier sonneteers wrote such general and unspecific sonnets that it is almost possible to replace a sonnet by one poet with that by another. Shakespeare's sonnets, in contrast, cannot be substituted by those of any other poet; the situations described are unique to Shakespeare.

The poet in Shakespeare's sequence addresses the young man on the subject of marriage (a topic unheard of in earlier sequences) and is almost disinterested in attitude. He expresses no view on exactly whom the young man might wed: any woman would do. His interest is only in the young man, and women are there only to provide potential mates for him. Shakespeare transplants the traditional situations of courtship (absence from the beloved, solitude, jealousy) and applies them not to a woman but to the young man. Furthermore, those sonnets addressed to a lady (those concerned with the Dark Lady) emphasise the negative aspects of sexuality:

> Th' expense of spirit in a waste of shame
> Is lust in action
>
> (sonnet 129)

Shakespeare's extension of the situation of sonnet sequences allows him to parody stylistic conventions of the genre. The poet in his sequence plays a number of different roles (adviser, artist, lover, betrayed friend), and included among these is the role of the detached, almost cynical realist who can invert conventions and highlight their emptiness. Sonnets such as 'Shall I compare thee to a summer's day' (18) and 'My mistress' eyes are nothing like the sun' (130) are deliberate parodies of the traditional comparisons used in earlier sonnets. Inventions like these are only possible through Shakespeare's development of the situations within the sequence. Sonnet 20, on the other hand, uses the device of addressing the young man in order to include some surprising and sophisticated bawdy: a different means of extending the range of variety of the sequence.

Thus Shakespeare is able to use the apparent limitations of the sonnet to great effect and, indeed, some of the strengths of his sequence come from his awareness of the potentials within sonnet conventions.

Part 5

Suggestions for further reading

The text

BOOTH, STEPHEN (ED.): *Shakespeare's Sonnets*, Yale University Press, New Haven and London, 1977. This is the text used in these Notes. Possibly over-ingenious in finding sexual references.

BURTO, WILLIAM (ED.): *The Sonnets*, The Signet Classic Shakespeare, New American Library, London, 1964. This includes an introduction by W. H. Auden as well as selected criticism.

DOVER, WILSON J. (ED.): *The Sonnets*, Cambridge University Press, London, 1967. An edition not widely respected by other critics, prepared when the eyesight of the editor was failing.

INGRAM, W. G. and REDPATH, T. (EDS): *Shakespeare's Sonnets*, University of London Press, London, 1964. This edition includes a valuable key to word-play in the sonnets, as well as a glossary.

KERRIGAN, JOHN (ED.): *The Sonnets and The Lover's Complaint*, Viking Press and Penguin, London and New York, 1986.

WELLS, STANLEY (ED.): *Shakespeare's Sonnets and The Lover's Complaint*, The New Clarendon Shakespeare, Clarendon Press, Oxford, 1985.

Other works by Shakespeare

ALEXANDER, P (ED.): *William Shakespeare: The Complete Works*, Collins, London and Glasgow, 1951; paperback edition, HarperCollins, Glasgow, 1994. A convenient single-volume edition of Shakespeare's complete works with a reliable text and a brief but informative introduction. The works most relevant to the sonnets are probably *The Merchant of Venice, Twelfth Night, Love's Labour's Lost, The Two Gentlemen of Verona* and *Timon of Athens*.

General works on Shakespeare

There are many general works on Shakespeare, of which the following are useful and, at present, up to date:

CAMPBELL, O. J. and QUINN, E. G. (EDS): *A Shakespeare Encyclopaedia*, Methuen, London, 1966. Arranged alphabetically; deals with Shakespeare's life, works and times.

HALLIDAY, F. E.: *A Shakespeare Companion 1564–1964*, Penguin Books, Harmondsworth, 1964.

LLOYD EVANS, G. and LLOYD EVANS, B.: *Everyman's Companion to Shakespeare*, Dent, London, 1978. Includes a useful glossary. It attempts to sort out some of the facts of Shakespeare's life and distinguish them from the myths and legends that have grown up.

MUIR, K. and SCHOENBAUM, S. (EDS): *A New Companion to Shakespeare Studies*, Cambridge University Press, London, 1971. Contains eighteen articles on a variety of topics relevant to the study of Shakespeare.

Dictionaries and glossaries

The standard reference work on the meaning of English words in the past is the *Oxford English Dictionary*. However, for students the glossary in *Everyman's Companion to Shakespeare* may suffice. In addition the following is a convenient source of information:

ONIONS, C. T.: *A Shakespeare Glossary*, Oxford University Press, London, 1911, revised by Robert D. Eagleson, 1986.

Another useful reference book is:

BAYLEY, PETER: *An A·B·C of Shakespeare*, (Longman York Handbooks) Longman, Harlow, 1985. New edition, 1993.

Criticism

A great deal of criticism has been written on sonnets in general and on Shakespeare's sonnets in particular. The following is a useful selection:

BOOTH, S.: *An Essay on Shakespeare's Sonnets*, Yale University Press, New Haven and London, 1969. Particularly concerned with the formal structure within the sonnets.

CRUTTWELL, P.: *The Shakespearean Moment*, Chatto & Windus, London, 1955. Sets Shakespeare's achievement in its contemporary context.

DUBROW, H.: *Captive Victors*, Cornell University Press, Ithaca and London, 1987. Includes sections on the narrative poems, as well as discussion of the sonnets.

FULLER, J.: *The Sonnet*, Methuen, London, 1972. A brief guide to the sonnet form.

JONES, P. (ED.): *Shakespeare, The Sonnets: A Casebook*, Macmillan, London, 1977. Particularly useful in discussing the relationships between the sonnets and Shakespeare's plays and in its selection of recent criticism of the sonnets.

KERNAN, A. B.: *The Playwright as Magician*, Yale University Press, New Haven and London, 1979. Includes a chapter on patronage and its relevance to the sonnets.

KOTT, J.: *Shakespeare Our Contemporary*, Methuen, London, 1965, 2nd revised edition, 1967. Includes a brilliant chapter on the sonnets and time.

LEVER, J.: *The Elizabethan Love Sonnet*, Methuen, London, 1956. The standard work on the Elizabethan sonnet.

MARTIN, P.: *Shakespeare's Sonnets, Self, Love and Art*, Cambridge University Press, London, 1972. Emphasises the theme of self-love, love of others, and love made permanent through art.

MUIR, K.: *Shakespeare's Sonnets*, Allen & Unwin, London, 1979. Includes commentary on the sonnets as well as background material and a survey of criticism.

PADEL, JOHN: *New Poems by Shakespeare: Order and Meaning Restored to the Sonnets*, Herbert Press, London, 1981. An interesting and innovative work proposing a re-ordering of the sonnets.

RAMSEY, P.: *The Fickle Glass*, AMS Press, New York, 1979. Three sections on the problems, the techniques and the meanings of the sonnets.

STIRLING, B.: *The Shakespeare Sonnet Order*, Cambridge University Press, London, 1969. Proposes a different order for the sequence from that of the 1609 edition. Its findings are interesting but inconclusive.

WINNY, J.: *The Master-Mistress, A Study of Shakespeare's Sonnets*, Chatto & Windus, London, 1968. Takes as its thesis a denial of the existence of the young man and emphasises the fictional aspects of the sonnet sequence.

The author of these notes

GEOFFREY RIDDEN is Head of Student Services at King Alfred's College, Winchester, and a former Course Director of the B.A. English degree programmes there. He was educated at West Hartlepool Grammar School and at the University of Leeds, and has held teaching posts at the University of Ghana, University College, London, the University of Durham, and Westfield College, London. He has also spent some time as Visiting Professor at the University of Wisconsin, Eau-Claire. He is the author of five titles in the York Notes series, and of the York Handbook *Studying Milton*. His most recent book is *Freedom and the English Revolution*, Manchester University Press, Manchester, 1986, which he co-edited with Roger Richardson. In 1987 he assumed the editorship of *The Hatcher Review*.

York Notes: list of titles

CHINUA ACHEBE
Things Fall Apart
EDWARD ALBEE
Who's Afraid of Virginia Woolf?
MARGARET ATWOOD
Cat's Eye
The Handmaid's Tale
W. H. AUDEN
Selected Poems
JANE AUSTEN
Emma
Mansfield Park
Northanger Abbey
Persuasion
Pride and Prejudice
Sense and Sensibility
SAMUEL BECKETT
Waiting for Godot
ALAN BENNETT
Talking Heads
ARNOLD BENNETT
The Card
JOHN BETJEMAN
Selected Poems
WILLIAM BLAKE
Songs of Innocence, Songs of Experience
ROBERT BOLT
A Man For All Seasons
CHARLOTTE BRONTË
Jane Eyre
EMILY BRONTË
Wuthering Heights
ROBERT BURNS
Selected Poems
BYRON
Selected Poems
GEOFFREY CHAUCER
The Franklin's Tale
The Knight's Tale
The Merchant's Tale
The Miller's Tale
The Nun's Priest's Tale
The Pardoner's Tale
Prologue to the Canterbury Tales
The Wife of Bath's Tale
SAMUEL TAYLOR COLERIDGE
Selected Poems
JOSEPH CONRAD
Heart of Darkness

DANIEL DEFOE
Moll Flanders
Robinson Crusoe
SHELAGH DELANEY
A Taste of Honey
CHARLES DICKENS
Bleak House
David Copperfield
Great Expectations
Hard Times
Oliver Twist
EMILY DICKINSON
Selected Poems
JOHN DONNE
Selected Poems
DOUGLAS DUNN
Selected Poems
GEORGE ELIOT
Middlemarch
The Mill on the Floss
Silas Marner
T. S. ELIOT
Four Quartets
Selected Poems
The Waste Land
HENRY FIELDING
Joseph Andrews
F. SCOTT FITZGERALD
The Great Gatsby
GUSTAVE FLAUBERT
Madame Bovary
E. M. FORSTER
Howards End
A Passage to India
JOHN FOWLES
The French Lieutenant's Woman
BRIAN FRIEL
Translations
ELIZABETH GASKELL
North and South
WILLIAM GOLDING
Lord of the Flies
OLIVER GOLDSMITH
She Stoops to Conquer
GRAHAM GREENE
Brighton Rock
The Heart of the Matter
The Power and the Glory

THOMAS HARDY
Far from the Madding Crowd
Jude the Obscure
The Mayor of Casterbridge
The Return of the Native
Selected Poems
Tess of the D'Urbervilles

L. P. HARTLEY
The Go-Between

NATHANIEL HAWTHORNE
The Scarlet Letter

SEAMUS HEANEY
Selected Poems

ERNEST HEMINGWAY
A Farewell to Arms
The Old Man and the Sea

SUSAN HILL
I'm the King of the Castle

HOMER
The Iliad
The Odyssey

GERARD MANLEY HOPKINS
Selected Poems

TED HUGHES
Selected Poems

ALDOUS HUXLEY
Brave New World

HENRY JAMES
The Portrait of a Lady

BEN JONSON
The Alchemist
Volpone

JAMES JOYCE
Dubliners
A Portrait of the Artist as a Young Man

JOHN KEATS
Selected Poems

PHILIP LARKIN
Selected Poems

D. H. LAWRENCE
The Rainbow
Selected Short Stories
Sons and Lovers
Women in Love

HARPER LEE
To Kill a Mockingbird

LAURIE LEE
Cider with Rosie

CHRISTOPHER MARLOWE
Doctor Faustus

ARTHUR MILLER
The Crucible
Death of a Salesman
A View from the Bridge

JOHN MILTON
Paradise Lost I & II
Paradise Lost IV & IX

TONI MORRISON
Beloved

SEAN O'CASEY
Juno and the Paycock

GEORGE ORWELL
Animal Farm
Nineteen Eighty-four

JOHN OSBORNE
Look Back in Anger

WILFRED OWEN
Selected Poems

HAROLD PINTER
The Caretaker

SYLVIA PLATH
Selected Works

POETRY OF THE FIRST WORLD WAR

ALEXANDER POPE
Selected Poems

J. B. PRIESTLEY
An Inspector Calls

JEAN RHYS
The Wide Sargasso Sea

J. D. SALINGER
The Catcher in the Rye

WILLIAM SHAKESPEARE
Antony and Cleopatra
As You Like It
Coriolanus
Hamlet
Henry IV Part I
Henry IV Part II
Henry V
Julius Caesar
King Lear
Macbeth
Measure for Measure
The Merchant of Venice
A Midsummer Night's Dream
Much Ado About Nothing
Othello
Richard II
Richard III
Romeo and Juliet
Sonnets
The Taming of the Shrew
The Tempest
Twelfth Night
The Winter's Tale

GEORGE BERNARD SHAW
Arms and the Man
Pygmalion
Saint Joan